HISTORY OF AMERICAN
SLAVERY

HISTORY OF AMERICAN
SLAVERY

Duncan Clarke

This edition published 1998 by
PRC Publishing Ltd,
Kiln House, 210 New Kings Road
London SW6 4NZ

Published in the USA by JG Press, 1998
Distributed by World Publications, Inc.,
455 Somerset Avenue, North Dighton, MA 02764

ISBN 1 57215 256 7

Printed in China

The photographs and drawings for this book were kindly supplied by the Hulton Getty Picture Collection,
with the following exceptions:

Duke University for pages 49, 81 (above and below), 84 (above and below), 85 (above and below), 92 (above and below), 93 (above
and below), 95, 96, 107, 141 (above and below), 142, 143 (above and below).

Pages 20 & 21, 31, 56 (below) and 57 (below) courtesy of Duncan Clarke.

Pages 22 and 127 courtesy of Bison Picture Library.

Page 121 courtesy of the Trustees of the Wedgwood Museum, Barlaston, Staffordshire, England.

Pages 71, 72, 88 (above and below) and 89 courtesy of the Public Record Office.

Crown Copyright material in the Public Record Office is reproduced by permission of
the Controller of Her Majesty's Stationery Office.

Images are reproduced by courtesy of the Public Record Office.

JACKET
All photos Hulton Getty.

The statistics on page 190 are taken from *Transformations in Slavery* by P. Lovejoy

Contents

1 Ancient Slavery in the Mediterranean World

The African slave trade, surely one of the most tragic and disturbing episodes in the history of mankind, had its origins in the intervention of forces from the civilizations that developed in the regions of the Mediterranean sea—today's Europe and the Middle East—into the arena of the more fragmented civilizations of sub-Saharan Africa. Africa became a source of slaves for the cultures of the Mediterranean world many centuries before the discovery of the Americas, but it was that discovery and the resulting shift in focus towards the Atlantic that prompted the culminating explosive growth in slavery with such tragic effect. Today our understanding of the nature of slavery tends to be framed by our impressions, gained perhaps as much from television and the cinema as from ancestral

memories, of the horrors of the transatlantic trade, the chains, the whips, and the overcrowded ships that brought so many traumatized Africans to the Americas. The images conveyed by *Roots* and more recently by *Amistad* however, although revealing and important, are only part of the picture. The slave experience of Africans in the Americas and elsewhere was much more varied and complex, while the nature of slavery in other cultures and at other times has

Below: Egyptian slaves under the direction of a supervisor drag a statue up the beach for placement inland. Slaves were present in substantial numbers in ancient Egypt, although much of the local population could be mobilized for large labor projects without reliance on formal systems of slavery.

Above: Queen Cleopatra of Egypt testing poison on slaves.
Painting by Colonel (1824–1889)

been marked by both similarities and differences to the American case. A few slaves, for example, were able to rise to positions of great personal wealth and power in some African societies, while others were rapidly incorporated into the family of their masters. Defining slavery in a way that encompasses these varying conditions over time is a complex academic issue about which debates still occur, but for our purposes we can regard it as the reduction of fellow human beings to the legal status of chattels, allowing them to be bought and sold as goods. The other aspects of their treatment generally follow from this fundamental distinction which we can see reoccurring again and again through the ancient history of the Mediterranean world, in Mesopotamia, in ancient Egypt, Greece, and Imperial Rome. Subsequently, slavery declined in importance as it was replaced by serfdom and other forms of restricted labor throughout most of Europe, but it remained a central feature of life in the Islamic societies of the Middle East and North Africa.

Slavery in the Ancient World: Babylon and Egypt

The Mesopotamian civilizations that developed from ancient Sumer in the fertile valleys of the Tigris and Euphrates (in present day Iraq,) beginning around 3500 B.C. until the fall of Babylon in 539 B.C., were based on elaborate city-states built largely with the use of slave labor. Slaves came from two main sources: men and women who were captured in the course of warfare (both against neighboring cities and further afield,) and citizens themselves who might fall socially to the status of slaves as a result of unpaid debts. Most slaves worked as laborers or

fulfilled other duties for one of the two dominant social institutions of these communities: the royal palace or the temple. Slaves were shaved and shackled in chains, and frequently branded with the sign of their owner. There is some evidence that locally-born slaves were obliged to work for only a limited period, in some cases three years, before their debt was discharged and they were set free.

Scholars have often noted that slavery was a marginal institution in ancient Egypt and did not really become widespread until the Late Period (after circa 700 B.C.) It is certainly the case that there was a large and important community of free commoners in Egyptian society, filling occupations such as merchants, interpreters, boatmen, craftsmen, and cattle herders, as well as the socially more important ranks of warriors and priests. However, there were also numerous people who, while not fulfilling the later legal definitions of slavery as applied in Greece or Rome, were certainly "unfree" laborers. These men and women were bound to specific areas of land and required to work for the benefit of its owner. Although in many cases this land-owner was the Pharaoh or the temple of one of the gods, a substantial amount of land was owned privately by officials, priests, warriors and other wealthy individuals. It is not clear what percentage of the population fell into this category, which is perhaps best summarized as serfdom, but it is thought to have included large numbers sentenced for criminal offenses, as well as

prisoners of war. Serfs could be transferred from one master to another, usually accompanying the land to which they were attached. Often these transfers took the form of gifts to temples.

Slavery as a recognized legal status, in which an individual could be bought and sold, emerged during the Late Period, as can be seen from a number of surviving documents recording contracts of sale. These slaves were legally prohibited from owning any property themselves. Although most are thought to have been foreigners captured in warfare or purchased from abroad, there is some evidence that a few native Egyptians were themselves obliged, perhaps through crime or absolute poverty, to become slaves. The limited evidence suggests also that the majority of slaves were well treated within a paternalistic relationship with their masters, and there are isolated reports of slaves rising to become highly ranked officials.

The Ancient Greeks

In contrast to the limited use of slaves in Egypt, the civilization that developed in Greece, and it successors around the shores of the Mediterranean, can be classified as slave societies. In other words, Greece and Rome were both cultures in which the institution of slavery was a fundamental aspect of social organization. Although these facts have long been apparent it is only in recent decades that scholars have documented in any detail the true nature of slavery in these two important ancient civilizations. Generations of writers before, mostly horrified by the activities of their forebears in the Atlantic slave trade, and embarrassed to report similar excesses in the Classical world which they revered as the font of European culture, tended to stress the paternalistic nature of ancient slavery and to downplay its pivotal role. In turn this rosy picture of ancient slavery itself served as an excuse and a justification for the apologists and pro-slavery enthusiasts of the ante-bellum American South.

Glimpses of the precarious position of slaves in ancient Greece can be found throughout some of the earliest sources, such as the epics of Homer. In *The Odyssey*, for example, the hero Odysseus, on his return from twenty years of travel and exile, greets kindly the old slave woman who nursed him. However the fate of the twelve slave-girls of the household was far different. Outraged to learn that they had allowed themselves to be seduced by the nobles who had taken advantage of his long absence in order to woo his abandoned wife Penelope, Odysseus forces them to clear away the bodies of their slaughtered lovers, then

Left: Slave power: Israelites in bondage in Egypt being exhorted to work by stick-wielding masters.

hands them over to his son Telemachus. Next, Homer records:

"He tied one end of a hawser to a pillar and passed the other about the roundhouse top, taking the slack up so that no one's toes could touch the ground. They would be hung like doves or larks in springes triggered in a thicket, where the birds think to rest, a cruel nesting. So now in turn each woman thrust her head into a noose and swung, yanked high in the air, to perish there most piteously. Their feet danced a little but not long."

Slaves who displeased their masters, as this mythological example makes clear, could be disposed of at will.

Slavery in ancient Greece was not regarded as an unfortunate but necessary evil; instead it was at the core of the political organization and self-conception of the Greek city states. The ideal of democracy, requiring self-government by communities of free men, rested on an understanding of the role of free citizens that has been described by one of the leading scholars of ancient slavery, Moses Finley: "The free man was one who neither lived under the constraint of, nor was employed for the benefit of, another; who lived preferably on his ancestral plot of land, with its shrines and ancestral tombs." In the technological and economic circumstances of the period, such an ideal inevitably required the acceptance of a large class of the "unfree." That these people should be slaves was taken to be natural and was universally accepted, even among the non-Greek "Barbarians" who made up a majority of the enslaved population—the author Xenophon makes the Barbarian king, Cyrus, announce the general view that, "it is a law established for all time among men that when a city is taken in war, the persons and the property of the inhabitants thereof belong to the captors."

The great philosopher Aristotle's famous justification of slavery, in his book *Politics*, draws heavily on this argument that slavery is a natural and generally accepted proposition, but also advances what we today would regard as a claim based on a supposed racial or ethnic distinction between the innate qualities of Greeks and Asiatic peoples. He argued that while the people of Europe had spirit but lacked skill and intelligence, they therefore remained free but backward. Those of Asia had skill and intelligence but lacked spirit and were therefore uniquely suited to being subjects and slaves. Only the Greeks, who as an intermediate culture combined the qualities of both spirit and intelligence, made natural rulers. How the self-styled heirs to Greek culture, in a slave trading Europe many centuries later, must have relished those words.

There were actually two distinct groups of people whom we would regard as slaves in Greek society. The first were the Helots, whole communities of Greek origin, most notably the Laconians, who were held in permanent

subjection by the forces of Sparta. These people were obliged to cultivate the land and hand over a large proportion of the produce to their masters. Far more widespread however, were the chattel slaves held by citizens throughout the Greek and Hellenistic world. There is little reliable evidence on which to base any estimate of the numbers of slaves in Greek communities, although it seems clear that they were at least a substantial minority. There are occasional references to single notable individuals owning several thousands of slaves, although this was far from the norm. Plato stated that to own fifty or more slaves was to be a wealthy man. The physician Galen suggests in his writings, that in his city of Pergamon in the second century A.D. there were 40,000 slaves out of an adult population of around 120,000, but it is not clear how far this may be useful as a guide to earlier periods.

Rather more is known about the sources of Greek slaves. We have already noted that it was generally accepted that prisoners of war were a legitimate source of slaves. Prisoners taken in the course of battle could meet any one of a number of fates. They might be immediately executed, they might be ransomed or set free, they could be incorporated into the victorious army, or they could become slaves. The choice rested with the victors and seems to have depended on the nature of the victory and the sentiments felt towards the captives. If they were to become slaves it was normal for the prisoners to be sold to professional slave traders who accompanied armies to battle for this purpose, rather than becoming the property of the soldiers themselves. A similar range of fates generally

Above: A slave works on a farm in Ancient Rome. Slaves used in agriculture were settled alongside a class of non-slave dependent tenants, called *coloni*, who, along with free peasants, provided the bulk of the rural labor force in most areas.

awaited the civilians—including the women and children —of a captured town, and while some of its slaves might now be freed, the majority were simply transferred to an uncertain new ownership. Although the Greeks fought most of their battles against other Greeks, the majority of their slaves were of non-Greek origin. There was a certain amount of reluctance expressed over holding Greeks as slaves, leading many to be ransomed and many others to be sold away to non-Greek markets.

Both Greeks and non-Greeks in the Mediterranean also lost their freedom by falling into the hands of pirates who were endemic throughout much of the region. Sicilian and Cretan pirates in particular are recorded as having supplied tens of thousands to the great slave market at Delos. Other important sources of slaves included the natural reproduction of the existing slave population, purchase from trade with non-Greek sources, the disposal of unwanted babies, and the enslavement of insolvent debtors. Large scale slave markets became established at Chios, Samos, Ephesus, Cyprus, and Athens.

Although there is much evidence for the good treatment of slaves and for their incorporation into Greek households on a paternalistic basis, as servants, housemaids, nurses, etc., it remains the case that in legal terms they were chattels at the absolute disposal of their masters. Most were allowed and even encouraged to marry, but these marriages had no status in law and families could be separated at will. Masters had and frequently exploited, absolute rights of sexual access to both male and female slaves from the earliest times. Castration was a punishment frequently applied to recalcitrant male slaves and slaves called on to give evidence in court were liable to be tortured, sometimes even taking the place of their master.

Nevertheless, there is also evidence that many slaves worked alongside freemen in much the same occupations. The dangerous and oppressive labor of mining silver and other metals, was, along with domestic servitude the only occupation performed exclusively by slaves. The army, law, and politics were reserved for free men, but all other tasks, including that of civil officials, could be performed by both slaves and freemen. Temples owned large quantities of slaves, responsible for maintaining the venerated buildings and in some cases, for sacred prostitution. Elsewhere, in large enterprises, whether rural farms or urban craft workshops, there were slaves at all levels, including the managerial. Surviving records of the workforce involved in the fifth century B.C. construction of the temple (known as the Erechtheum) on the Athenian Acropolis note that there were twenty skilled slave craftsmen working alongside twenty-four Athenian citizens and a number of foreigners. Many slaves of this type simply worked

alongside their masters, who collected a share of their wages. Slaves worked as craftsmen potters, occasionally even depicting their own craft and workshop, in which case they would follow the established convention of depicting a "slavish" appearance or posture. Manumission, or the granting of freedom, sometimes took place in return for some exceptional or faithful service, or on the death of the owner, although the majority of slaves were passed on, along with the master's other property, to his heirs. Other slaves were able to raise sufficient money to purchase their freedom. Freedmen could not become citizens of Greek polities, remaining members of a group with restricted rights, known as "metics."

The Roman Empire

If slavery pervaded Greek society, it was their successors to the dominance of the Mediterranean world, the Romans, who took the institution onto a dramatic new scale. It has been suggested that a conservative estimate would put the

Below: In Victorian England the image of Pope Gregory in the slave market, where he is said to have remarked that the youths from England on sale were "*non Angli sed Angeli*" (not Angles but Angels), was extremely popular. In fact this sentimental image of the pope as an early abolitionist has little historical foundation and it is reported that in A.D. 595 he sent a priest called Candidus to Britain to buy pagan slave boys to work on monastic estates.

number of slaves in Italy at the conclusion of the Republican era at around two million. A few wealthy individuals owned extremely large numbers of slaves. A noble Roman lady, Melania, who decided in the year A.D. 404. that she and her husband would renounce their vast worldly wealth and live in Christian poverty, is reported by contemporary accounts to have freed some 8,000 of her slaves, leaving many thousands of others who were unwilling to accept freedom to be sold with her numerous estates. While this is clearly an exceptional and doubtless exaggerated tally, far more common was the example of a prefect in Rome during the reign of Nero who had a staff of 400 slaves at his townhouse alone. The unfortunate slaves of the Urban Prefect, Pedanius Secundus, fell victim to a long-standing Roman law which demanded that in the event of the murder of a master within his house, all of his slaves should be put to death regardless of their individual part in the crime. There was some unrest among the urban poor of the city on this occasion which prompted the Senate to debate the justice of such a law. It was upheld and the sentence of death carried out, to serve as a deterrent to others. If wealthy senators like the murdered prefect (apparently killed through jealousy over an affair with a male slave) had numerous slaves, the advantages of slave ownership were not restricted to the rich. At the other end of the social sale it was also accepted practice for

ordinary citizens to have one or more slaves to assist with household tasks or work on the land. In Antioch, for example, even the very poor owned one or two slaves.

Where did all these vast numbers of slaves come from? The primary source was the capture of huge numbers of men, women, and children in the course of warfare. Like the Greeks, the Romans took it for granted that a high proportion of these captives should be sold into slavery, unless there was some overriding political reason for treating them more leniently. In the course of his conquest of Gaul, Julius Caesar took some one million prisoners, while in 167 B.C., 150,000 captive Epirotes were brought back to Rome for sale after a single battle. There were also wars beyond the frontiers of the Empire supplying a further stream of captives, and as in Greece, kidnapping and piracy were a constant threat. Then there was the natural reproduction of the existing slave population, with any children born to slave mothers becoming slaves themselves, regardless of the status of the father. There are some reports of masters who deliberately encouraged slave women to have children by rewarding them with exemption from work after a number of children. Since slave marriages and kin relationships had no legal status these children were, of course, available for sale. Finally, there were two further sources which seem surprising to us today. Many poor people, unable to sustain themselves as tenant farmers, or facing famine beyond the Empire's borders, would voluntarily offer themselves and their families for sale as slaves, knowing that at least they would be guaranteed a minimal sustenance. Secondly there was the widely practiced custom known as "exposing," whereby unwanted babies were simply left outside. Although no doubt many of these children simply died of hunger and exposure, it was accepted that the majority would be picked up and reared for sale into slavery. This practice, which effectively severed any ties the child had with his former family, was an important method of restricting family size, used by the rich to reduce the number of children entitled to a share of the family wealth, as well as by those too poor to feed another infant. The majority of Rome's slaves therefore came from internal sources or from warfare in the Empire's provinces in Europe and Asia Minor. Although there are records of some sub-Saharan African slaves, and African people were of course enslaved in the Roman provinces of Egypt and North Africa, there is no evidence that slaves were a significant component of the trade that already criss-crossed the Sahara along routes still dotted with ancient rock paintings of charioteers.

Spartacus

The brilliant leadership and personal heroism of the rebel leader Spartacus made him a hero for both contemporary Roman authors and, in the twentieth century, for Hollywood film makers. Plutarch tells of his revolt:

"A certain Lentulus Batiatus had a school of gladiators at Capua, most of whom were Gauls and Thracians. Through no misconduct of theirs, but owing to the injustice of their owner, they were kept in close confinement and reserved for gladiatorial combats. Two hundred of these were planned to make their escape, and when information was laid against them, those who got wind of it and succeeded in getting away, seventy-eight in number, seized cleavers and spits from some kitchen and sallied out. On the road they fell in with wagons conveying gladiators' weapons to another city; these they plundered and armed themselves. Then they took up a strong position and elected three leaders. The first of these was Spartacus, a Thracian of Nomadic stock, possessed not only of great courage and strength, but also in sagacity and culture superior to his fortune . . .

"To begin with, the gladiators repulsed the soldiers who came against them from Capua, and getting hold of many arms of real warfare, they gladly took these in exchange for their own, casting away their gladiatorial weapons as dishonorable and barbarous. Then Clodius the praetor was sent out from Rome against them with 3,000 soldiers, and laid siege to them on a hill which had but one ascent, and that a narrow and difficult one, which Clodius closely watched; everywhere else there were smooth and precipitous cliffs. But the top of the hill was covered with a wild vine of abundant growth, from which the besieged cut off the serviceable branches, and wove these into strong ladders of such strength that when they fastened at the top they reached along the face of the cliff to the plain below. On these they descended safely . . .

"Spartacus then fought his way northwards, intending to disperse his troops to their homes beyond the Alps. They refused to leave, and the army headed back to the tip of Italy, planning to cross over to Sicily. They failed to find ships, and Licinius Crassus moved against them.

"Spartacus retired to the mountains of Petelia, followed closely by Quintus, one of the officers of Crassus, and by Scrophas, the quaestor, who hung upon the enemy's rear. But when Spartacus faced about, there was a great rout of the Romans, and they barely managed to drag the quaestor, who had been wounded, away into safety. This success was the ruin of Spartacus, for it filled his slaves with over-confidence. They would no longer consent to avoid battle. Spartacus saw the necessity that was upon him and drew up his whole army in order of battle.

"In the first place, when his horse was brought to him, he drew his sword, and saying that if he won the day he would have many fine horses of the enemy's but if he lost it he didn't want any, he slew his horse. Then pushing his way towards Crassus himself through flying weapons and wounded men, he did not indeed reach him, but slew two centurions who fell upon him together. Finally after his companions had taken to flight, he stood alone, surrounded by a multitude of foes, and was still defending himself when he was cut down."

Left: Pope Saint Calixtus I, Pope in A.D. 218–222, originally a slave and later martyred.

basis, while passing on much of their revenues to their masters. In exceptional cases these slaves were even sent on trading missions abroad on behalf of their masters. At the same time, the virtually exclusive use of slaves in any large scale enterprise made slave production a primary source of income for the elite slave-owning classes. Numerous manuals of instruction for slave owners by Roman writers reveal something of the complexities that were felt to be involved in managing these slave labor forces so as to achieve optimum returns while minimizing the expenses of their maintenance. Cato, for example, writing in 170 B.C., suggested that when a new cloak or tunic was issued to his slaves, the old garment should be collected for possible reuse.

A substantial proportion of the slave population, however, was not directly employed in productive activities at all; instead, they made up the vast households of servants ministering to the needs of the wealthy elite. Such people often maintained large numbers of slaves in each of their numerous town residences and country estates. Each of these slaves would, where possible, be assigned a highly specialized individual task, as Roman aristocrats regarded it a sign of poverty to have the same slave responsible for two household duties. As well as domestic servants, cooks, children's wet nurses, and tutors, household slaves pursued varying tasks such as hairdressers, singers and dancers, physicians, librarians, and accountants. As might be expected the constant attendance of so many dependant and sexually exploitable slaves played a key role in the complex family relationships of the Roman elite. Satirists frequently mocked Roman ladies who revealed their concern at the sexual excesses of their husbands, while it became an accepted practice for divorced or widowed older men to take on a freed slave as his recognized concubine. Any children of such a relationship, while they might expect to be looked after well, would be excluded from the inheritance of their legitimate siblings.

The possibilities for financial accumulation made available by the system of *peculium*, or independent businesses, together with the variety of sentimental ties that inevitably grew between masters and slaves within households, contributed to the large number of slaves who were able to purchase or be granted their freedom. In a notable difference from the custom in Greek cities, it was possible for these freedmen to achieve Roman citizenship, although there were periodic upsurges of concern about the numbers who were doing so. Laws were passed to

Although much has been made of the use of chained and brutally treated slave gangs in the working of large *latifundia* agricultural estates in areas of Italy and Sicily, most scholars now agree that these were exceptional measures intended to control a rapid influx of large numbers of prisoners of war rather than the normal mode of slave use throughout the Empire. Slaves were used on a smaller scale in agriculture, but in many cases they were settled alongside a class of non-slave dependent tenants, called *coloni*, who, along with free peasants in most areas provided the bulk of the rural labor force. Unlike slaves, these people could be taxed directly and were a vital source of state revenues. Many of them were themselves owners of a few slaves to supplement their own labor. As in Greece, Roman slaves could be employed in a huge variety of occupations and provided the permanent labor force for virtually all types of productive employment larger than that of families of craftsmen or women. Once again, slaves and the free could work side by side at the same trade. The Roman system known as *peculium* even allowed slaves to operate small scale separate enterprises, working as craftsmen or shopkeepers on an individual restrict manumission of slaves to certain categories, such as those over the age of thirty, but these were of only passing impact. However, despite the favorable circumstances often achieved by quite substantial numbers of individual slaves, as a class they were virtually devoid of legal rights and could be subjected to an array of extremely harsh judicial punishments, in addition to their vulnerability to the whims and caprices of their masters.

Branding on the face was a common punishment for runaway slaves. The use of chains, whippings, and beatings was commonplace and even the reforms—supposedly alleviating slave conditions under the influence of Christianity—published under the Emperor Constantine, absolved masters from responsibility for any deaths that might result from such treatment (they did however threaten punishment for those who killed slaves by, among other means, poisoning, hanging, or excessive torture.) The judicial use of torture on slaves was standard procedure in many cases. The most notorious incident of capricious cruelty was reported by Seneca, who recorded that Caesar was obliged to intervene when one of his friends ordered that a young slave boy who accidentally smashed his master's favorite crystal cup should be killed by being thrown into a pond where he kept huge and voracious fish.

Not surprisingly considering the harsh circumstances facing at least some Roman slaves, and the sporadic influxes of huge numbers of prisoners of war, revolts and insurrections were a pervasive concern to the Roman authorities. Mostly, however, the problem was confined to small-scale episodes hardly distinguishable from outbreaks of banditry by runaways and impoverished free men. There were though, a small number of major slave rebellions in Italy and Sicily that posed a serious challenge to the state. Some 6,000 slaves of mostly Syrian origin, outraged by particularly brutal treatment, rebelled in Sicily in 135 B.C. Conflict continued over several years, during which the rebels captured many towns and killed large numbers of Roman citizens before order was restored. A second large uprising in Sicily in 104 B.C. also took several years and an

Below: Twenty-two different tortures supposedly inflicted on Christian slaves in the Barbary States of North Africa in the 1600s. Although slaves were castrated to produce eunuchs for service in harems (a procedure which apparently had a 90 percent mortality rate), this representation of slave life has little relation to the complex and varied roles of slaves in Islamic societies.
From* Histoire de Barbarie *by Dan, published in 1637.

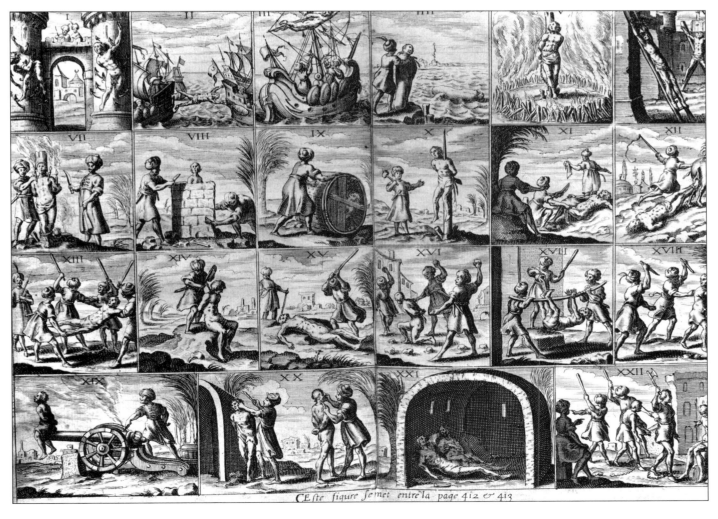

CE fte figure fe met entre la page 412 e 413

invading army of 17,000 Roman legionnaires to suppress a slave force said to have amounted to 30,000 fighters.

The best known slave rebellion of the ancient world however was that which occurred in 73 B.C. on the Italian mainland. Spartacus, a Thracian who escaped with a small group of followers from a gladiatorial training school at Capua, rapidly established a growing band of Thracian, Celtic, and German slaves who plundered and devastated a large area of Italy. The first two modest forces sent against him by the Roman authorities were totally defeated, requiring the despatch from Rome of a major army under the leadership of Crassus, and the recall of a second force lead by Pompey from Iberia. Trapped between these powerful armies, Spartacus was killed in battle in 71 B.C. and 6,000 of his captured followers were executed by crucifixion along the Appian Way. More common than these attempts to overthrow the state was the participation of often quite large numbers of slaves in the numerous civil wars that occurred in both the Republican and Imperial eras. Those slaves who were astute or fortunate enough to be fighting on the victorious side were generally rewarded with freedom, while the losers were savagely punished.

The Carthaginians, for many centuries the rivals of Rome in the western reaches of the Mediterranean, were also a slave-using society. Slaves were employed in the cultivation of large agricultural estates in the hinterland, while Carthaginians were active as slave traders throughout the western Mediterranean. The inhabitants of the Balearic islands reportedly would exchange three or four male slaves for a single woman. Many of the slaves in Carthage were of Berber origin, but the presence of sub-Saharan

Above: The Chinese were sold as slaves by the Mongols after Genghis Khan's thirteenth century conquest.

Africans has also been documented by archaeologists. Dark skinned Africans were among the Carthaginian soldiers captured during an unsuccessful invasion of Sicily in the fifth century B.C.

Europe after the Fall of Rome

Scholars have recently recognized that the previously accepted view of the end of slavery in Europe is over-simplistic. It had been accepted that slavery in Europe was replaced as the main system of restricted labor by the spread of serfdom in the aftermath of the gradual collapse of Roman imperial authority from around the fifth century A.D. Whilst it is true that the rights of Roman tenants, or *coloni*, were increasingly restricted, and the collapse of central authority made the poor ever more reliant for protection on local lords, it is no longer clear that there was any sudden decline in the incidence of slavery accompanying the rise of rural feudalism. The spread of Christianity may have resulted in occasional measures that sought to restrict excessive ill treatment of slaves or the break up of slave families, but these were of limited impact and as was the case during the Atlantic slave trade centuries later, the Catholic church can hardly be said to have opposed slavery in principle or practice. For example in A.D. 595 Pope Gregory the Great sent a priest called Candidus to Britain to buy pagan slave boys to work on monastic estates. The historian Marc Bloch has noted that by the early Middle Ages slavery was still widespread in Europe. At the time of the compilation of the Domesday book in eleventh century England, some ten percent of the population were slaves, as were ten to fifteen percent in thirteenth century Genoa.

The most important source of slaves in medieval Europe was the coast of Bosnia on the eastern shores of the Adriatic sea. The word "slave" and its cognates in most modern European languages is itself derived from *sclavus* meaning "Slav", the ethnic name for the inhabitants of this region. As Christianized kingdoms established their authority throughout most of Europe, the rulers of these new states, while certainly not opposed to slavery, did seek to prevent the export of their own population as slaves, primarily no doubt because taxable agricultural peasants were in fact their own main source of revenue. Slave traders were obliged to turn their attention to more remote frontier regions which still lacked stable government. For various reasons, including the harshness of the terrain and endemic warfare among local clans, Bosnia proved the most convenient and long-lasting of these slave-supplying regions. Whichever clan gained a temporary upper hand was always willing to sell its captured rivals in exchange for the goods of the Mediterranean world in the markets of the ancient Romanized city of Ragusa (present day Dubrovnik.) From there Slavs were shipped as slaves by Venetian merchants, to supply new markets in the Islamic world and the continuing demand for household servants in parts of Europe, especially the city states of northern Italy and Catalonia. For the Islamic world, Slavs provided the major source of slaves in the 250 or so years between the defeat at the battle of Poitiers in A.D. 732. that forced the consolidation of their dramatic conquests across North Africa and the Iberian peninsula, cutting back the flow of war captives, and the expansion of the import of black Africans across the Sahara from around A.D. 1000.

Although Christians in Europe were becoming increasingly concerned about the propriety and legal validity of enslaving fellow Christians, particularly if they were to be sold to Muslims, the unfortunate Bosnians remained legitimate targets because they were associated with a heretical sect, the "Bogomils," which flourished in the region in the thirteenth century. They could therefore be regarded as pagan, and were even issued with notarized certificates to this effect before being sold. The trade continued until the conquest of the region by the Ottoman Turks in 1463, which prompted one final wave of captives. The effective closure of the last major source of slaves on the European continent thus coincidentally took place at the same time as the Portuguese explorations of the West African coast which were to open up the second and most devastating route for the exploitation of Africans as slaves.

Below: Russian serfs beaten by Cossacks on the Don. Serfdom, which was abolished by Alexander II in 1861, perpetuated the legal subjugation of peasants that had declined elsewhere in Europe with the ending of feudalism.

2 Slavery in African Society

In the early decades of the thirteenth century A.D., the Mande warrior Sundiata established a vast kingdom stretching between the upper course of the Senegal river and the bend of the Niger, controlling the southern access to a network of ancient trade routes that linked sub-Saharan Africa to the Mediterranean world. The wealth of this kingdom, based on its strategic position straddling both overland and riverine trade routes, and especially on its access to the gold fields of Wangara, became fabled throughout Europe and the Middle East following the pilgrimage made to Mecca by Sundiata's grandson Mansa Musa in 1324. With a huge caravan of followers, Mansa

Musa, the third king of Mali, rode into Cairo preceded by 500 slaves, each carrying a staff of solid gold weighing 500 mithqal (a mithqal was about an eighth of an ounce). Although trade with sub-Saharan Africa had been

Below: Slaves were owned in large numbers by chiefs and nobles in the Kongo kingdom.

Right: A print from 1800 showing idealized depictions of the dress of three Kongo women. On the left was the artist's impression of slave attire. Kongo was a major source of slaves exported to the Americas, and slaves also played a key role in the local economy.

Dreſs *of the* Women *at* Kongo.

Left: Weaving in the Yoruba town of Iseyin, Nigeria. In the past the production of cloth for the local rulers and for inter-regional trade often involved the employment of large numbers of slaves in the growing and processing of cotton and indigo. Elsewhere in West Africa, weaving itself was often the work of subjugated groups.

Above: A drawing of the plant of genus *Indigofera* which provides the basis of a dye color between blue and violet. In the nineteenth century and earlier, slaves were used in Kano and several other areas of Africa to grow and process indigo for the local weaving industries.

established for thousands of years, it being an important source of ivory and other luxury goods to both ancient Egypt and Carthage, the conjunction of Islam, gold, and slaves in Mansa Musa's famous pilgrimage, characterized a new, more intensive phase. Trans-Saharan contacts with the Islamic world since around 1000 A.D. were soon to be supplemented by the expansion of European seaborne trade along the West African coast. Africa was now linked into worldwide trading networks—the rapidly expanding Atlantic arena, the more established region of the Mediterranean, and, along its eastern shores, an ancient Indian Ocean trade network that extended from the Red Sea as far as Imperial China. Each of these routes played its part in the tragic history of Africa's involvement with slavery. In order to understand that history it is necessary to consider the nature of slavery within Africa itself and to explore the impact the slave trade had on the evolution of African societies.

The subject of slavery within Africa, and of the active participation of Africans in the export of slaves, is one that

Olaudah Equiano describes his capture

Equiano, from the Igbo region of Nigeria, was a slave in Barbados, Virginia, and England before buying his freedom in 1766. Taking the name Gustavus Vassa he became a prominent opponent of the slave trade and published a well-known account of his life. Below he describes his capture.

"One day, when all our people were gone out to their works as usual and only I and my dear sister were left to mind the house, two men and a woman got over our wall, and in a moment seized us both, and without giving us time to cry out or make resistance they stopped our mouths and ran off with us into the nearest wood. Here they tied our hands and continued to carry us as far as they could till night came on, when we reached a small house where the robbers halted for refreshment and spent the night. . . . I was now carried to the left of the sun's rising through many different countries and a number of large woods. The people I was sold to used to carry me very often, when I was tired, either on their shoulders or on their back. I saw many convenient well-built sheds along the roads at proper distances, to accommodate the merchants and travelers who lay in those buildings along with their wives, who often accompany them; and they always go well armed . . . All the nations and people I had hitherto passed through resembled our own in their manner, customs and language: but I came at length to a country the inhabitants of which differed from us . . . Thus I continued to travel, sometimes by land, sometimes by water, through different countries and various nations, till at the end of six or seven months after I had been kidnapped I arrived at the sea coast.

"The first object which saluted my eyes when I arrived on the coast was the sea, and a slave ship which was then riding at anchor and waiting for cargo. These filled me with astonishment, which was soon converted into terror when I was carried on board. I was immediately handled and tossed up to see if I were sound by some of the crew, and I was now persuaded that I had gotten into a world of bad spirits and that they were going to kill me. Their complexions too differing so much from ours, their long hair and the language they spoke (which was very different from any I had ever heard) united to confirm me in my views and fears at the moment that, if ten thousand worlds had been my own, I would exchange my condition with that of the meanest slave in my own country. When I looked round the ship too and saw a large furnace or copper boiling, and multitude of black people of every description chained together, every one of their countenances expressing dejection and sorrow, I no longer doubted of my fate; and quite overpowered with horror and anguish, I fell motionless on the deck and fainted. When I recovered a little I found some black people about me, who I believed were some of those who had brought me on board. Of those white men with horrible looks, red faces, and loose hair, one brought me a small portion of spirituous liquor in a wine glass, but being afraid of him I would not take it out of his hand. One of the blacks therefore took it from him and gave it to me, and I took a little down my palate, which instead of reviving me, as they thought it would, threw me into the greatest consternation at the strange feeling it produced, having never tasted any such liquor before.

"I now saw myself deprived of all chance of returning to my native country or even the least glimpse of hope of gaining the shore, which I now considered as friendly; and I even wished for my former slavery in preference to my present situation, which was filled with horrors of every kind, still heightened by my ignorance of what I was to undergo. I was not long suffered to indulge my grief; I was soon put down under the decks, and there I received such a salutation in my nostrils as I had never experienced in my life: so that with the loathsomeness of the stench and crying together, I became so sick and low that I was not able to eat, nor had I the least desire to taste anything. I now wished for the last friend, death, to relieve me; but soon, to my grief; two of the white men offered me eatables, and on my refusing to eat, one of them held me fast by the hands and laid me across I think a windlass, and tied my feet while the other flogged me severely. I had never experienced anything of this kind before, and although, not being used to the water, I naturally feared that element the first time I saw it, yet nevertheless could I have got over the nettings I would have jumped over the side, but I could not; and besides, the crew used to watch us very closely who were not chained down to the decks, lest we should leap into the water: and I have seen some of these poor African prisoners most severely cut for attempting to do so, and hourly whipped for not eating. This indeed was often the case with myself. In a little time after, amongst the poor chained men I found some of my own nation, which in a small degree gave ease to my mind. I inquired of these what was to be done with us; they gave me to understand we were to be carried to these white people's country to work for them. I then was a little revived, and thought if it were no worse than working, my situation was not so desperate; but still I feared I should be put to death, the white people look and acted, as I thought, in so savage a manner; for I had never seen among my people such instances of brutal cruelty, and this not only shown towards us blacks but also to some of the whites themselves. One white man in particular I saw, when we were permitted to be on deck, flogged so unmercifully with a large rope near the foremast that he died in consequence of it; and they tossed him over the side as they would have done a brute. This made me fear these people the more, and I expected nothing less than to be treated in the same manner. I could not help expressing my fears and apprehensions to some of my countrymen: I asked them if these people had no country but lived in this hollow place (the ship): they told me they did not, but came from a distant one . . . At last, when the ship we were in had

got in all her cargo, they made ready with many fearful noises, and we were all put under deck so that we could not see how they managed the vessel. But this disappointment was the least of my sorrow. The stench of the hold while we were on the coast was so intolerable loathsome that it was dangerous to remain there for any time, and some of us had been permitted to stay on the deck for the fresh air; but now that the whole ship's cargo were confined together it became so crowded that each had scarcely room to turn himself. This produced copious perspiration, so that the air soon became unfit for respiration from a variety of loathsome smells, and brought on a sickness among the slaves, of which many died, thus falling victims to the improvident avarice, as I may call it, of their purchasers. This wretched situation was again aggravated by the galling of the chains, now become insupportable, and the filth of the necessary tubs, into which the children often fell and were almost suffocated. The shrieks of the women and the groans of the dying rendered the whole scene of horror almost inconceivable. Happily perhaps for myself, I was soon reduced so low that it was thought necessary to keep me almost always on deck, and from my extreme youth I was not put in fetters. In this situation I expected every hour to share the fate of my companions, some of whom were almost daily brought upon deck at the point of death, which I began to hope would soon put an end to my miseries . . .

"One day, when we had a smooth sea and moderate wind, two of my wearied countrymen who were chained together (I was near them at the time,) preferring death to such a life of misery, somehow made through the nettings and jumped into the sea; immediately another quite dejected fellow, who on account of his illness was suffered to be out of irons, also followed their example; and I believe many more would very soon have done the same if they had not been prevented by the ship's crew, who were instantly alarmed. Those of us that were the most active were in a moment put down under the deck, and there was such a noise and confusion amongst the people of the ship as I never heard before, to stop her and get the boat out to go after the slaves. However two of the wretches were drowned, but they got the other and afterwards flogged him unmercifully for thus attempting to prefer death to slavery. In this manner we continued to undergo more hardships than I can now relate . . . (until) the island of Barbados."

has aroused considerable controversy, and is still the subject of both academic and political dispute. At the time of the slave trade, European apologists for the exploitation of Africa, argued, without troubling to explore any evidence, that slavery was the natural condition of African labor, and they even claimed that the slavers were benefiting the African captives by saving them from a worse fate. abolitionists, in contrast, while accepting that slavery was indeed widespread in Africa, argued that this was a direct result of the pernicious impact of the slave trade on previously tranquil societies. For members of the African Diaspora, those peoples of African ancestry now dispersed around the world as a result of the slave trade, it is understandably distressing to realise that fellow Africans in the ancestral homeland may well have contributed to the suffering of the enslaved. Moreover, it is all too easy for conservative commentators, such as the apologists for slavery at the time, to dwell on this African involvement as if it somehow excuses or lessens the guilt attached to the horrors of European and American exploitation of African peoples. Reinterpreting history all too often becomes a weapon for fighting today's battles, played out through the idiom of racism that is one of the most tragic legacies of the slave trade era.

Yet, despite differences in emphasis and detail, both Euro-American and African scholars now generally accept both that slavery was widespread in Africa, and that Africans played an active part in enslaving other Africans, for local use and for export. In itself, this African involve-

ment is not surprising. The global perspective from which African solidarity becomes a relevant issue is itself largely a product of the twentieth century, emerging in the aftermath of colonialism and the awareness of common interests that the continuing problems of racism in the Diaspora have engendered. Within Africa itself, at the time of the slave trade no such perspective was possible. Instead there were the immediate economic, strategic, and political interests of the powerful, which as in so many other parts of the world, found expression through the exploitation of the weak. Scholarly controversy still continues as historians and anthropologists argue over the precise nature of, and trajectories taken by, the history of slavery in different regions of Africa, and on the consequences of that involvement on issues such as the population impact and the pace of economic development. While there is insufficient space here to explore the details of these often obscure debates, the rest of this chapter will provide an introduction to some of the major issues.

Defining African Slavery

The term "slave" in European languages, and the legal and social traditions that framed the terms of enslavement in

Below: Arabs riding their camels in the Sahara. Many thousands of enslaved Africans died of hunger and thirst in the long trek across the Sahara before they could reach the slave markets of the Islamic world. A nineteenth century traveler on one regular route described the tracks as being lined with skeletons.

Europe and America, arose from the long history of slavery in the Mediterranean world which we explored in the previous chapter. At the same time, our own picture of slavery is generally informed by images of plantation slavery as it developed in the Americas. Moreover, our understanding of the apparently contrary situation of freedom is itself bound up with ideas about the role of individuality and liberty that have developed comparatively recently in European history. None of these can be uncritically transferred to the consideration of slavery in the very different and varied societies that developed in Africa. Slavery is, as we have seen in Europe, not the only form of "unfree" labor, and there has been considerable debate about which, if any, of the various more or less restricted conditions in which people found themselves in many African societies are best characterized by the use of the term "slavery."

In a controversial but influential paper the anthropologists Miers and Kopytoff argued that slavery in Africa should be understood as a relative concept, opposed not to freedom but to integration within the lineage or other social institutions prevailing in a particular society. Thus while a newly purchased slave far from home was a chattel, over time it was often possible, to an extent that varied between different societies, to become increasingly integrated into the society of the captors, with the degree of integration generally increasing with subsequent generations. In many, but by no means all cases, by the second or third generation, no social distinction was officially made

Above: Timbuktu, a center of trade and Islamic scholarship. The Islamic African states and cities of the Sahel incorporated large numbers of slaves and other people of servile status, many of them working farms organized in slave villages.

between those of slave and free born origin. This was particularly so when slave women and children were incorporated into their master's extended family. Influenced by this approach Paul Lovejoy, a leading historian of African slavery has argued that "slavery was fundamentally a means of denying outsiders the rights and privileges of a particular society so that they could be exploited for economic, political, and economic purposes." The precise rights, responsibilities, and treatment of individuals of slave origin varied considerably from one African society to another, depending on both local traditions and the purpose for which slaves were required. The specific histories of slavery in each of a myriad of African societies are subjects that continue to be the focus of historical research and about which much remains to be understood. Underlying this diversity however, two broad types of African slave systems have been identified which, however oversimplified, provide a basis for understanding both the character of African slavery, and the way it changed over time.

In general terms, much of pre-colonial Africa, whether ruled by small centralized states or by more dispersed localized mechanisms of authority, was characterized by what has been called a "lineage mode of production." Kinship, and relations of seniority expressed in terms of age and gender, were the main principles of social organization, with senior men controlling access by their juniors to both women and land. Women's labor was essential for the productive use of land and, of course, for the reproduction of the society. The relative success of individual male elders in these societies was dependant on their ability to maintain and increase the size of their kinship group or section, and hence the quantity of land, game, wild products, etc that it could exploit. Since in most areas more land for cultivation was readily accessible, the primary constraint on the group's production was the number of dependent kin and followers that it could attract and maintain. Successful leaders were those who could expand their own immediate family by marrying additional wives, as well as feed their dependants, reward the younger men with wives of their own, and mobilize sufficient armed men to fend off attacks in those areas where state authority was lacking. Such men, or in a few cases women, could expect to attract clients dissatisfied with prospects in their own group. The primary role of slavery in lineage societies of this type was to provide an alternative means for the leaders to increase the size, and therefore the productive and reproductive potential of their group of dependants. It was often cheaper to purchase slave women than to obtain wives from neighboring

groups through the elaborate and costly procedures of bridal payments. Furthermore, the women purchased, along with any children they had subsequently, lacked any other kin group to serve as an alternative source of support or divide their loyalties. Young children could also be rapidly assimilated. Male slaves were usually less in demand (a factor that was reflected in the generally lower price paid for male slaves in the domestic markets) but they too could be used to supplement the kin group on occasion.

Whether incorporated completely into the host society or maintained as a subservient group, slaves in lineage societies were one type of dependant among others, usually working alongside other dependant group members such as young men, junior wives and pawns. Pawnship was a widespread practice whereby dependant people, often children, could be transferred, on a more or less temporary basis, as security for an outstanding debt. Slaves performed the usual range of productive tasks allocated to men and women in these societies, such as farming, gathering wild produce, hunting, and a range of craft techniques from pottery making to weaving. In cotton growing areas women slaves were an important part of the labor force required in spinning cotton prior to weaving. Once purchased, slaves were unlikely to be resold unless they proved unusually uncooperative and recalcitrant, but in times of famine or other crisis, recently acquired slaves were particularly vulnerable. In some cases central author-

Far right: Agadez, Niger, an important starting point for trans-Saharan caravans taking slaves to the North.

Right: The Islamic slave trade across the Sahara involved an estimated average of some 5,000 people a year between A.D. 650 and 1600.

Right: The Tuareg of the central Sahara were feared raiders and caravan traders with with west African ports.

Far right: The salt mines to the north of Lake Chad were worked by slaves in appalling conditions over a period of many centuries.

ities or slave raiding groups exacted tribute from villages in their path in the form of slaves, and then too it would be the recently acquired, and hence least integrated, people who were most at risk.

The nature of the data available for the reconstruction of the history of African societies does not really provide much evidence by which to judge the antiquity of this form of slave holding. Some historians have argued that since slave ownership provided the main means of accumulating wealth in cultures where the individual ownership of land was not found, some version of this type of slavery must have been an extremely longstanding feature. Others, though, have noted that the ready availability of large quantities of captive women and children in particular must have increased as the frontiers of organized slave catching were pushed ever deeper by the demands of the Atlantic trade. Therefore, the export trade must have been, at the very least, a major factor in promoting domestic slave use within lineage societies. Before this, they argue, slavery can have been at most a marginal feature of African social organization.

It seems even more probable that both the market network, and the mechanisms for the capture and transport of large quantities of slaves necessary to supply the export trade, were a major factor in the emergence of the second major form of slave use within Africa, which has been called the "slave mode of production." Without entering into the disputed technicalities of this term, a "slave mode of production" can be said to have existed in those areas

where these established mechanisms of enslavement and distribution fed a regular supply of new slaves into organized systems of productive labor, providing a large proportion of the wealth of the slave-holders involved. These included the use of slaves in plantation based agriculture, which became quite widespread in many areas including the Senegambia region, the densely populated countryside around such Hausa weaving centers as Kano, and in the Omani Arab-controlled clove plantations of Zanzibar. Major plantation crops included cotton, indigo, millet, and pepper, along with other staple vegetables. Usually slaves were required to work most of the day for five or six days a week and also to provide the bulk of their own food from separate plots. As in the Americas, whipping and the use of chains were established practice. Male slaves were provided with a wife at the master's discretion, with any children remaining his slaves, although it was rare for them to be sold away.

Other forms of a "slave mode of production" were less widespread, but included productive systems which developed around the exploitation of slaves in mining, for example in the Asante and gold mines, in large-scale production of textiles, and in livestock rearing. While many of the cheaper male slaves were destined for export at the hands of Europeans, in areas of the savannah belt remote from the network of routes that fed slaves into the Atlantic trade, male slaves were particularly cheap as both local lineage needs and the Islamic export trade favored the purchase of women and children. The low price of male slaves

in these areas contributed to their use both as slave warriors in organized troops, which of course expanded the capacity of their masters to acquire still more slaves through raiding, and as agricultural workers settled in slave villages on land allocated by the slave-holders. Slave warriors were common and a long established tradition in both Muslim and non-Muslim areas. Perhaps the best known were the *tyeddo*, bands of brightly dressed long haired warriors nominally the slaves of Muslim Wolof rulers and powerful matrilineages in the region of what is now Senegal.

While it would be too simplistic to see the history of slavery in Africa as an unidirectional move from lineage-based systems to those using a "slave mode of production," it seems clear that this form of slave use did become both more widespread and more intensive as Africa became increasingy integrated into worldwide trading networks—the most intense period of slave exports taking place in the first half of the nineteenth century. The nature of this change, which scholars have called a transformation in African slave-using societies, varied with the specific local circumstances of each region. Ironically these developments received a further boost as the effective abolition of

the Atlantic export trade in the following decades led to a switch in overseas mercantile interest towards so-called "legitimate trade" in such products as hardwoods, rubber, and palm oil. Since this both reduced the price payable for slaves in Africa and increased the demand for the products of their labor, a marked expansion of slave use in plantation agriculture occurred throughout the continent.

Islam and the African Slave Trade

In our revulsion at the cruelties of the Middle Passage to the Americas it is often forgotten that the export of Africans as slaves across the Sahara began many centuries before the Atlantic slave trade and continued for several decades longer. When the famous Arab traveller, Ibn Battuta, one of the earliest writers to leave any account of Africa south of the Sahara, crossed the desert on his return from Mali in the fourteenth century, he accompanied one caravan which was transporting 600 women slaves by a route via the oasis towns of Air, Tuat, and Sijilmasa. The hardships of these long marches across the desert were considerable, and much later travelers reported that the routes were lined with the parched skeletons of those who succumbed to exhaustion and thirst along the way. Any

Right: A map of Africa showing slave routes in the late nineteenth century. For earlier periods, routes to the west coast from Senegambia down to Angola were also important.

Above: Drummers in the Yoruba town of Oyo play for Ogun, the deity of iron and warfare, at a hunters' festival. Ogun was one of the most important deities to have survived the Middle Passage and became a key figure in the Afro-Carribean religions of Vodou, Santeria, and Candomble.

Left: A collection of animal skulls used by customers for medicinal purposes on a market stall in Mali. Aspects of African traditional medicinal practices were maintained by African-American slaves and their descendants in the Americas.

miscalculation or misfortune over the supply of water could easily result in the loss of the entire caravan, the traders sometimes   perishing alongside their captives.

Sources that allow an estimate of the total numbers exported by Arab slavers are somewhat limited, but the historian, Paul Lovejoy, has suggested that between A.D. 650 and 1600 an average of some 5,000 people a year were involved, making a very rough total estimate of about 7.25 million. A further 1.4 million followed in the years between 1600 and 1800, while the nineteenth century represented a culminating peak in the annual volume at around 12,000 per year, making a total of 1.2 million for the century as a whole (and an estimated 9.85 million in all). These figures should be compared with an estimated total for the Atlantic trade made by the same historian of 11,698,000 people between A.D. 1450 and 1900. Slaves were also shipped across the Red Sea directly to Arabia, and via the Indian Ocean to both the Persian Gulf and, in smaller numbers, to India. The total numbers involved in the Red Sea and Indian Ocean trades were somewhat smaller but also very substantial. Lovejoy's estimates for these areas total some 4.1 million with, once again, the largest annual numbers from the first part of the

nineteenth century. This trade also, with the notable exception of some Portuguese involvement in the area of Mozambique, and of eighteenth and nineteenth century French exports to islands that were under their control in the Indian Ocean, was largely conducted by Muslims.

The Islamic world was the inheritor of far older ideas about the role and use of slaves, and they filled much the same roles as domestic servants, administrative officials, and soldiers, as in the pre-Islamic Middle East. Nevertheless the laws of Islam did modify both the grounds of possible enslavement and the legal status of slaves. In particular, fellow-Muslims were not supposed to be enslaved. Women

Below: Images such as this depiction of an Arab slave raid in Africa were circulated by the abolitionist movement throughout the nineteenth century to draw attention to the continuing human costs of slave raiding and the need for European intervention to suppress it.

Right: Late nineteenth century photograph showing a group of chained slaves captured from a trader, guarded by a colonial soldier.

Below right: A late nineteenth century print showing starving slaves on board an Arab dhow captured during naval patrols to suppress the slave trade in the Indian Ocean.

Above: Throughout the nineteenth century slaves were imported into Zanzibar by its Omani Arab rulers to work on clove plantations.

Right: For many hundreds of years large numbers of sub-Saharan African women were incorporated as slaves into families throughout the Arab cities of North Africa and the Middle East.

slaves were often readily incorporated into Islamic societies as concubines or more rarely as wives, their children becoming free. Those concubines who bore children for their master could no longer be sold, becoming legally free on his death. Male children were often trained for military or administrative service, with the prospect of emancipation and incorporation into the host society for the successful. A few men of slave origin subsequently rose to

positions of considerable wealth and power, although this was by no means the norm. Women not taken into harems, along with the smaller number of adult male slaves purchased, were worked hard at menial tasks and seldom had the opportunity to reproduce themselves. Large numbers of young boys were castrated in order to become eunuchs, an operation that is said to have had a survival rate of around one in ten.

The combined effect of all these factors was a steady demand for slaves throughout the Islamic world, which had to be met from wars, raids or purchases along the borders with non-Islamic regions. Although some of these slaves came from Russia, the Balkans, and central Asia, the continuing expansion of Islamic regimes in sub-Saharan Africa made black Africans the major source. Unlike in the Americas however, ideas of race were rarely important in

determining a continued servile status, although claims to Arab descent in the paternal line could be important, for example in the Swahili trading ports of East Africa. As cities and states with Muslim governments were established across the savannah belt and down the East African coast the customs and traditions of Muslim slave use spread ever further afield. Well beyond the areas of direct Islamic governance, Muslims dominated long distance trade routes throughout much of western and eastern Africa, with substantial Muslim communities developing at key points on trade networks. Islamic conventions regarding the conditions of slavery were diffused with them, modifying aspects of older local practices.

Sources of Slaves in Africa

How did people in Africa become enslaved in the vast numbers needed to supply both the huge export trade and the steady local demand? As in other slave-supplying regions of the world, the key method was through the enslavement of captives taken in warfare. Men captured in the course of fighting, as well as men, women, and children taken in their conquered villages or towns, were routinely enslaved in many regions. Sometimes the younger men might have the opportunity to join the ranks of their attackers, while many of the women and children would be taken into the households of the leading soldiers, but the remainder who were of suitable age could be sold on to slave traders. While African wars were rarely, as the eighteenth century abolitionists argued, fought solely in order to capture slaves, the prospect of valuable captives certainly added weight to the usual strategic and political motives.

Organized slave raiding was often on such a regular and sustained level that it can hardly be distinguished from warfare. Many Muslim powers in particular, for example the Hausa cities of northern Nigeria, sent out raiding parties to gather slaves from their pagan neighbors every dry season. In central Africa groups of raiders—such as the notorious Imbangala war bands—spread terror and destruction over vast areas. Smaller scale raiding shaded off into the equally pervasive threat of kidnapping, where straying children or solitary travelers risked falling prey to the slavers. They could then, as the Igbo slave boy Olaudah Equiano later recounted in his celebrated memoirs, be carried far from home before the alarm was raised.

These two major mechanisms of enslavement operated from outside each society. Most people risked enslavement primarily from attackers or kidnappers beyond their community, however that was locally defined. Similarly

Right: A street scene in Cape Verde: Portuguese colonists took slaves from Africa to work sugar plantations on these islands in the early phase of the Atlantic trade.

their own warlords, chiefs, or other slave traders generally directed their own activities towards outsiders. There were however less commonly occurring circumstances whereby individuals could be enslaved and sold away by their own people. Usually this applied only to persistent criminals and debtors, although others could also be at risk in times of extreme famine or other crisis. Moreover, whatever the local conventions defining who was a legitimate target for enslavement, the weak and vulnerable were always at risk of these rules being flouted by the powerful. Finally there are cases of large numbers of people being enslaved as a result of the activities of oracles and other religious agencies. The best known example of this was a famous oracle, called Ibinukpabi, but known to Europeans as the "Long Juju," maintained by the Aro who controlled the marketing of slaves among the Igbo and Ibibio peoples throughout a large area of south-east Nigeria. Many of those who disappeared after they had traveled long distances to consult this fearsome oracle in his skull-lined cave were in fact promptly sold by the Aro to the European ships on the coast.

The Impact of the Slave Trade on African Societies

Aside from the incalculable personal tragedies that engulfed those caught up in the slave trade, the effects on African societies of a trade in people, that by the nineteenth century had spread to draw captives from all but the most isolated regions, have proved remarkably hard to assess. Huge numbers of young men, women and children were lost to the continent altogether, while as many more were forcibly shifted to labor in hostile conditions. Moreover, to the many millions exported we have to add the millions more who died in the course of slave raids, in the arduous marches to the coast or across the desert, or from disease in the crowded pens of the merchants on the coast. Famines caused by wars and raids, and the consequent loss of able-bodied labor must have claimed numerous further victims.

Quantifying the direct and indirect effects is complicated by the fact that they were extremely unevenly distributed. Some regions were continually raided for slaves over many centuries, other nearby regions did much of the raiding, while still others shifted from one camp to the other over time. Nevertheless the majority of scholars are broadly agreed that, as we might expect, the slave trade did have a significantly adverse demographic impact on Africa. Assessing the long-term economic consequences are still more complex, particularly as they

Left: Following the abolition of slavery throughout British colonies, large numbers of Indians were imported as indentured servants, both to the Caribbean, and to South and East Africa. Here Indian women work on a Natal sugar plantation.

became entangled with the later effects of colonialism and the continuing economic imbalances of the post-colonial era. Some have even suggested that the market mechanisms, flow of goods, and wider involvement of Africa in global trade networks that were promoted by the slave trade may have even boosted the economic growth of the continent. All of these ends however could have been achieved at far less human cost by trade in other goods, and this approach ignores the evidence of the long standing existence of quite sophisticated long-distance trade networks and currency systems in many parts of Africa independent of slave trading. Any marginal benefit must have been far outweighed by the disruption and loss of productive potential caused by the draining of population.

However, the fact that it is now evident that the trade was seriously harmful to Africa as a whole does not mean that African rulers and merchants were somehow forced or otherwise coerced into participating. Until the end of the nineteenth century Europeans generally lacked the will or the means to engage in effective military action beyond the range of the heavy guns of their ships. The Portuguese did intervene a few times in local wars in Benin and Angola but without any obvious reward. Even the massive Morrocan invasion force that crossed the Sahara at the end of the sixteenth century and brought down the Songhai Empire ultimately failed to secure the riches that were hoped for. More normally both Europeans and Arabs relied on the cooperation and support of local rulers and were careful to follow the often laborious and expensive preconditions they laid down before trade could take place. There were numerous incidents where uncooperative Europeans, even those in ships or forts, were killed or starved into submission. Their backers, whether merchants or governments, had little option if they wanted renewed access to lucrative trade, but to send a replacement to negotiate new terms. As we shall see when we consider the organization of the Atlantic trade in the next chapter, African rulers laid down, often in considerable detail, precisely what they wanted in return for the slaves they had to sell, and the traders had to accept or try their luck elsewhere. Nor, as is sometimes suggested, did they become dependent on European goods such as guns, and trapped into adverse trade in that way. Guns, although important for prestige, were rarely used in African warfare until the nineteenth century when the trade in slaves was already approaching an end. Of course, the local rulers and merchants, like their counterparts far in the interior who operated the slave supply networks, did not themselves suffer the harmful effects of the trade, in so far as they were apparent at the time. Instead they profited, using the luxury goods and weapons gained from the Europeans to boost their prestige and increase their power still further.

3 The Atlantic Trade and the Growth of Slave Society in the Americas

The Atlantic slave trade with all its tragic consequences, did not result from any coherently planned programme to tap the labor potential of Africa in order to exploit the abundant natural resources of the newly discovered continents of the Americas. Instead, although it was rooted in the ready acceptance of the institution of slavery by the pioneers of Atlantic exploration, it emerged in a piecemeal and haphazard fashion as new areas of the Atlantic world were opened up to settlement and the commercial viability of new crops and sources of precious metals were established. Slavery was, as we have seen, well established in both the Christian and Muslim societies of the Mediterranean world. Within Africa itself, various forms of "unfree" labor were widespread. Yet within decades of Portuguese ships first reaching the West African coastline in the fifteenth century the largest enforced population movement the world has seen was already underway. Over the next four centuries some ten million or more Africans were shipped under the most horrendous conditions imaginable, to live, work, and die in a new and alien world. Contrary to popular perception, scholars now estimate that only some six to seven percent of these Africans were landed on the North American mainland. Before we turn in the next chapter to a consideration of the slave experience of these people in North America, we will look here at the emergence of slavery in the Atlantic arena, the organization of the trade, the shared traumas of the Middle Passage across the Atlantic, and at the slave societies of the Caribbean and South America.

Portuguese Exploration and the Beginnings of the Atlantic Trade

The Portuguese, situated at the far western boundaries of the Mediterranean world, yet benefiting both from their long experience of sailing well beyond the relatively calm seas of the Mediterranean to trade with ports in Britain and northern Europe and from their intimate knowledge

Left: Prince Henry of Portugal, (1394-1463) known as Henry the Navigator, popularly credited with instigating the Portuguese exploration of the West African coast in the fifteenth century. Slaves were taken on these voyages and sold for use in Portugal.

Right: Following Christopher Columbus's discovery of the Americas in 1492, the native population was decimated by disease, making new sources of labor essential to the exploitation of the colonies.

of Islamic North Africa, were exceptionally well placed to exploit the new possibilities for Atlantic exploration made possible by advances in maritime technology in the fourteenth and fifteenth centuries. Inspired as much by the prospect of short term commercial gains as the long term goal of outflanking the Islamic rulers of the Middle East by discovering a sea route to the Indies and the gold mines of "Ethiopia," Portuguese—and to a lesser extent Catalan and Castillian Spanish—ships began to raid the Moroccan coast and the newly rediscovered Canary Islands in the fourteenth century. These voyages bought back trade goods including animal hides, wood products and dyestuffs, but also an increasing number of slaves obtained by raiding.

Permanent colonization of the Canary Islands began in 1402–1405, setting a pattern for the exploitation of other Atlantic islands with the establishment of agricultural production using the forced labor of Africans. After the Portuguese captain, Gil Eannes, successfully returned from a voyage beyond Cape Bojador in 1434, breaching a previously much feared frontier of the known world, successive voyages pushed further down the African coast, making contact for the first time with populous regions and established local kingdoms. The gold producing regions of the Gold Coast were reached around 1470, with regular trade beginning further east with the kingdom of Benin in 1485–86, and Diego Cão, on a voyage sponsored by the crown, making contact with the kingdom of Kongo in the early 1480s. By 1488 Bartolomeu Dias reached the southern tip of the African continent, opening up

Portuguese trade into the Indian ocean. The islands (all uninhabited except for the Canaries) discovered in the course of this exploration, notably Madeira, the Cape Verdes, and São Tomé, were first exploited by the gathering of wild products, but it soon became apparent that with the use of slave labor from the Canaries and the African mainland they would support rich harvests of sugar, wine, and other highly valued goods.

Thus even before Columbus's voyage of 1492 revealed the presence of a previously unknown continent, the Portuguese and Spanish were using African slaves in plantation agriculture on the Atlantic islands. Other slaves, estimated at around 1,000 per year, were being brought back for sale in Lisbon. At first the Portuguese simply seized their captives in raiding parties sent ashore, but they soon found that African forces using canoes were able to offer surprisingly successful resistance. In 1447 for example, the Danish captain and most of the crew of a Portuguese vessel were killed by local people in a naval battle off the island of Gorée. After these early setbacks the practice of negotiating with local African rulers and winning their consent to engage in trade of both slaves and goods became the norm throughout the history of the Atlantic trade. The Portuguese found well-established commercial markets and trade networks which they could tap into and extend. For example they bought slaves in Kongo and indigo dyed textiles in both Benin and Ijebu (a Yoruba-speaking kingdom in south-western Nigeria) and resold both in exchange for gold on the Gold Coast. It seemed a

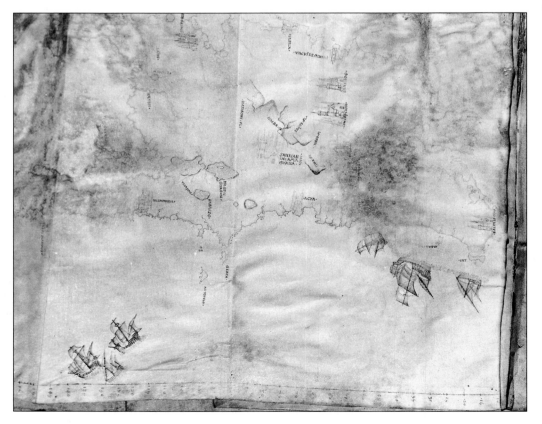

Right: A map drawn by Columbus, showing the newly discovered island of Hispaniola, now Haiti and the Dominican Republic, which was to become one of the largest importers of slaves in the Americas.

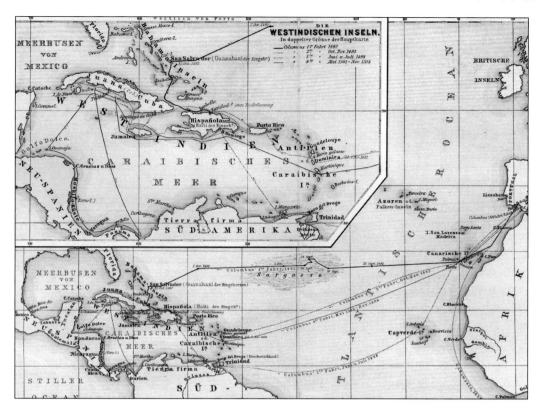

Left: A German map tracing the voyages of Christopher Columbus (1446–1506) to the West Indies and the Caribbean Sea.

natural extension of these developments to turn to African labor to exploit the agricultural potential and mineral wealth of the colonies the Portuguese were establishing in Brazil, and the Spanish throughout their vast new possessions in the Caribbean and the American mainland. In 1510 King Ferdinand of Spain authorized the purchase of 250 Africans in Lisbon to be carried to his territories in New Spain. The Atlantic slave trade was underway.

Africans were not the only source of "unfree" labor available to the colonists of the Americas. Both Native Americans and Europeans were also used. Labor from these sources however was to prove neither as suitable nor as effective in the majority of cases. The Native American population of the Caribbean and South America, and rather later, of North America, was devastated by a combination of disease, the exceptional brutality of the colonists, and the destruction of existing systems of agriculture and commerce. In most areas population numbers collapsed to a fraction of their former levels. Although in the sixteenth century there was a thriving slave trade in prisoners captured from the unconquered parts of the Caribbean and during the conquest of Mexico, and numerous more localized systems of enslavement persisted elsewhere, Spanish laws and the pressure of missionaries prevented the enslavement of the majority of the subjugated Native American populations. Moreover, most Native Americans slaves lacked the skills needed and were unable to adjust to the patterns of labor required of them. Although they continued to be employed as servants and were integrated as a subject labor force in the colonial economies of

Spanish America and Brazil they were not a substitute for African slaves. Often Native American laborers worked on the same plantations as African slaves but performed only seasonal labor and unskilled tasks.

The immigration of Europeans, either as free workers or as indentured servants, was a potential second source, particularly once the British, Dutch, and French had established colonies in the Caribbean and North American mainland. However, the available supply of such workers was limited—no European countries at this period had the surplus of urban poor that was to fuel mass emigration to the Americas in the nineteenth and early twentieth centuries. Indentured servants, who signed contracts obliging them to work for a period of years (usually between three and seven) in return for their passage and board on arrival, as well as a small plot of land on expiry of the contract, were comparable in cost for masters in the West Indies with slaves bought from Africa. In 1695 an indentured servant cost Jamaican planters in the region of $15–25 plus transportation fare, while a slave cost around $30. Many thousands of Europeans did come to the Caribbean as indentured servants, but mortality rates through exposure to new diseases and often harsh frontier labor conditions were high. Moreover, the planters found it inconvenient to release the survivors and grant them land, thereby creating growing numbers of troublesome smallholders. It was far better from their perspective of economic self interest to import Africans who were not only relatively more resistant to tropical diseases but could be denied all rights and kept in slavery indefinitely.

Advice to Slave Traders

During the 18th century numerous merchants and officials engaged in the slave trade published accounts of their experiences for the advice and guidance of future traders. Although the callous racism that pervades these texts is frequently distressing, books such as the one written by John Atkins, a naval surgeon, provide an invaluable guide to the perceptions and practices of the traders themselves.

"In the Windward Coast, Gambia, Sierraleon, and Sherbro Rivers may be reckoned chief; the African company having Factors and Settlements there. Less noted, but more frequented by private Ships this part of Guinea, are Cape Mount, and Montzerado, Sesthos River, Capes Palmas, Apollonia, and Tres Puntas. A number of others intervene, of more or less Trade; which it is their Custom to signify at the sight of any Ship by a Smoke, and is always looked on as an Invitation to Trade; but as each is alterable among them from the Chance of War, the Omission shews they decline it, or are out of Stock.

"This Change of Circumstance found on different Voyages, proceeds from weak and bad Governments among themselves, every Town having their own Cabiceers or ruling Men, (or it may be three or four in Confederacy) all so jealous of the others Panyarring, that they never care to walk even a mile or two from home without Fire-Arms; each knows it is their Villanies and Robberies upon one another that enables them to carry on a Slave-trade with Europeans . . .

"Cape Coast: The Factory consists of Merchants, Factors, Writers, Miners, Artificers and Soldiers; and excepting the first Rank, who are the Council for managing Affairs, are all of them together a company of white Negroes, who are entirely resigned to the Governor's commands, according to the strictest Rules of Discipline and subjection; are punished (Garrison fashion) on several Defaults with Mulcts, Confinement, the Dungeon, Drubbing, or the Wooden Horse . . . tho' the Salaries sound tolerable in Leadenhall-Street (50 to 90 $\pounds$ per Ann a Factor; 50 an Artificer) yet in the country here, the General (for the Company's good) pays them in Crackra, a false Money which is only current upon the spot . . .

"In the Area of this Quadrangle (of Cape Coast Castle) are large Vaults, with an iron Grate at the Surface to let in Light and Air on those poor Wretches, the Slaves who are chained and confined there till a Demand comes. They are all marked with a burning iron, DY, Duke of York . . .

"Within the Castle is a Smith's Shop, a Cooperage, Store-houses, a Chappel, and Houses for the Officers and Servants. The General's Lodging communicates with the Chappel; a capacious Hall, which serves to preach and dine in' pray or drink, serve God or debate or Trade; hence they can overlook what the Company's Servants are doing . . .

"First, on the Timing of a Cargo: this depends at several places much on Chance, from the fanciful and various Humours of the Negroes, who make great demands one Voyage for a Commodity, that perhaps they reject next . . .

Secondly, Of the Sorting, this may be observed in general; That the Windward and Leeward Parts of the Coast are a substantial Part of Windward Cargoes. Crystals, Orangos, Corals, and Brass-mounted Cutlasses are almost peculiar to the Windward Coast; as are brass Pans from Rio Sesthos to Apollonia: Cowreys (or Bouges) at Whydah. Copper and Iron Bars at Callabar; but Arms, Gun-powder, Tallow, old Sheets, Coffons of all the various Denominations, and

English Spirits are everywhere called for . . .

The Sale of Goods At Sierraleon

	Gold Bars
1 Piece of Planes	10
2 771b Kettles	26
3 Pieces of Chintz	12
I piece of handkerchief Stuff	2
The Price of a Woman Slave	50
7 501b Kettles	20
5 Pieces of Brawls	10
1 piece of Ramal	4
1 Bar of iron	1
The price of a Boy Slave	35

Slaves: Slaves differ in their Goodness: those from the Gold Coast are accounted best, being cleanest limbed, and more docible by our Settlements than others; but then they are, for that very reason more prompt to Revenge, and murder the Instruments of their Slavery, and also apter in the means to compass it.

"To Windward they approach in goodness as is the distance from the Gold Coast; so, as at Gambia, or Sierraleon, to be much better, than at any of the interjacent places.

"To Leeward from thence, they alter gradually for the worse; an Angolan Negro is a Proverb for worthlessness; and they mend . . . till you come to the Hottentots . . .

"I have observed how our Trading is managed for Slaves, when obliged to be carried on aboard the Ship. Where there are Factories . . .we are more at large; they are by us in like manner, as our Brother Trade do Beasts in Smithfield, the Countenance, and Stature, a good Set of Teeth, Pliancy in their Limbs, and joints, and being free of Veneral Taint, are the things inspected, and governs our choice in buying . . .

"Whydah Slaves are more subject to Small-Pox and sore Eyes; other parts to a sleepy Distemper, and to Windward, Exomphalos's. There are few instances of Deformity any where; even their Nobles know nothing of chronicle Distempers, nor their Ladies, of the Vapours. Their flattish Noses are owing to a continued grubbing in their Infancy against their Mother's Backs."

Below: Prints, often circulated by Abolitionists, show the cramped sleeping position of slaves on board a slave ship, but cannot capture the horrendous conditions described by contemporary reports.

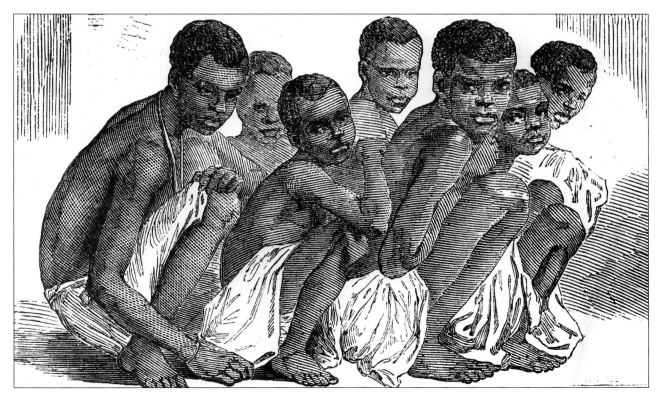

Slave Traders and the Slaving Nations

The history of the involvement of a succession of European powers and their colonies in the business of shipping Africans as slaves to the Americas is a complex one. It is inextricably bound up with far wider issues of the shifts in relative economic strength and maritime power of the participating nations, the vagaries of numerous European wars, changes in the attitude of governments towards issues such as regulated versus free trade, and the possibilities offered by the differing situations in their various colonies and bases in both Africa and the Americas.

Although Portugal and Spain pioneered the development of colonies in the Americas, the Spanish were prevented by the Treaty of Tordesillas, signed after Papal mediation in 1494, from establishing colonies in Africa. This left the Portuguese with a monopoly of the transatlantic trade until the closing years of the following century, while the Spanish colonies were reliant on purchasing slaves shipped by other powers. The Spanish Crown's attempt to regulate and profit from this position by the sale of a series of import license contracts, known as *asiento*, contributed to European rivalry over the trade while failing to furnish sufficient slaves to meet the virtually insatiable demands of her vast colonies. Although the Dutch vigorously attacked the Portuguese monopoly throughout the seventeenth century, the continued expansion in demand for slaves, and the overall growth of the trade meant that Portuguese slavers carried ever increasing numbers over the following centuries. Recent figures by Rawley, based on Philip Curtin's pioneering census indicate total shipments by the Portuguese to be in the order of 4.2 million Africans, rising from under a quarter of a million in the sixteenth century, to a peak of over 1.9 million in the eighteenth century, and a further 1.45 million in the nineteenth century before the trade was finally halted in the 1870s.

The far-reaching Dutch assault on the maritime empire of the Portuguese and Spanish came in the course of the Eighty Years' War (1568–1648). By the 1630s and 1640s Dutch naval superiority had allowed them to take both the Pernambuco sugar-plantation region of Brazil and important African slave supplying areas, including Gorée, the fort of El Mina in the Gold Coast and coastal regions of Angola, from the Portuguese. Although the Portuguese subsequently regained control of Brazil and the Angolan ports, the Dutch were able to take a substantial share of the slave trade. Among the Dutch colonies established in this period, including New Amsterdam, only Surinam on the South American mainland became a large slave-using economy, but the Dutch role as a major maritime power was secured. The relatively barren Dutch-controlled Caribbean island of Curaçao became a major entrepôt for the illicit supply of slaves to the French Caribbean and Spanish America. The Dutch scholar Johannes Postma has estimated the total number of Africans carried by the Dutch to be just under a half million.

French slave traders, based in the ports of Nantes, Bordeaux, La Rochelle, and Le Havre, carried slaves from Senegambia, the Windward Coast, the Bight of Benin, and Angola, to both French Caribbean colonies and the mainland of South America. French slave trading was

Below: A view of Lisbon in 1640. In 1510 King Ferdinand of Spain authorized the purchase of 250 Africans in the slave markets of Lisbon to be carried to his territories in New Spain. The Atlantic slave trade was underway.

Left: A burial ceremony for a Native American chief or priest in 1565. Although in the sixteenth century there was a thriving slave trade in prisoners captured from the unconquered parts of the Caribbean, during the conquest of Mexico, Spanish laws and the pressure of missionaries prevented the enslavement of the majority of the subjugated Native American populations.

Below: Europeans arrive on American soil in 1600, to be greeted by Native Americans, who extend a hand of friendship and the peace pipe to the strangers.

Above: Dutch colonial officer Peter Minuit (1580–1638) purchases Manhattan Island from Man-a-hat-a Native Americans, for trinkets valued at $24. *By Alfred Fredericks*

insignificant until the end of the seventeenth century, reaching a peak in the final decades of the eighteenth century, before the loss of her main slave using colony in Saint-Domingue in the 1790s, and French defeat in the Napoleonic war two decades later, brought an abrupt end. Over the century as a whole it is estimated that French slavers carried something over a million people, making it the third largest participant in the Atlantic trade. By far the largest number of French-imported slaves, along with numerous others bought by other slavers, went to labor in the sugar plantations of Saint-Domingue (present day Haiti). Astonishingly this single colony is now thought to have been the second largest importer of slaves after Brazil, taking nearly ten percent of the total. The French were also significant participants in a much smaller scale eighteenth century and early nineteenth century trade in slaves from Madagascar and South East Africa to plantation economies established on various small Indian Ocean islands.

Although British slave trading took place as early as the notorious voyages of John Hawkins in the 1560s, the organized participation of the British on any scale began with a series of companies granted successive royal charters to engage in slave trading and other African trade in the latter part of the seventeenth century. The Royal Africa Company, chartered in 1672, played a major role in maintaining the string of forts on the African coast and exported some 89,000 slaves between 1673 and 1689. After that

date the company's monopoly was increasingly challenged by new independent traders. Slavers from the ports of Bristol and Liverpool now overtook those based in London, although London remained both an important slaving port and the center of the European sugar trade. By the 1730s the British were the dominant slaving nation, a position they maintained until abolition in 1807. Between 1690 and 1807 they transported in the vicinity of 2.8 million African slaves.

Although the supply of provisions to the slave societies of the Caribbean had long been the economic mainstay of the colonies of New England, and the southern colonies were themselves of course based on slave labor, the direct participation of the states of North America in the transatlantic trade itself was relatively minor and of only about 50 years' duration. Beginning as late as 1760, American slave traders carried some 425,000 Africans, a large proportion of whom were landed in Brazil and Cuba. A smaller illicit trade to these two countries continued into the 1860s. The major U.S. slave trading ports were Newport, Providence, and Bristol, as well as Rhode Island,

Stowing Human Cargoes

An excerpt from the memoirs of Theophilus Conneau (published as *A Slaver's Log Book,* by R. S. Mott Inc.) records the procedure for loading as many slaves as possible:

"Two of the officers have the charge of stowing them. At sundown the Second Mate and Botswain descend, cat in hand, and stow the Negroes for the night. Those on the starboard side face forward and in one another's lap, vulgarly called spoon fashion. On the port side they are stowed with face aft; this position is considered preferable for the free pulsation of the heart. The tallest are selected for the greatest breadth of the vessel, while the short size and youngsters are stowed in the fore part of the ship. Great precaution is also taken to place those such as may have sores or boils on the side most convenient for their distemper. Tubs are also distributed on the sleeping deck and so placed that both sides have access. (The sick are never placed below.)

"This lower deck once full, the rest are stowed on the deck, which is prepared with loose boards to keep the water from under them; they are then covered in fair weather with spare sails and with tarpaulins in rainy nights. In this manner they are made to remain all night, if possible. This discipline of stowing them is of the greatest importance on board slavers; otherwise every Negro would accommodate himself with all the comfortability of a cabin passenger . . .

"Billets of wood are sometimes distributed to them, but as slaves shipped are often of different nations this luxury is not granted till well assured of the good disposition of the Negroes, as on many occasions slaves have been tempted to mutiny only by the opportunity at hand of arming themselves with those native pillows—indeed a very destructive missile in case of revolt.

"As it may appear barbarous that slaves should be made to lie down naked on a hard board, let me inform the reader that native Africans know not the use of mattresses . . . Therefore slaves cannot find great inconvenience in laying down on hard boards."

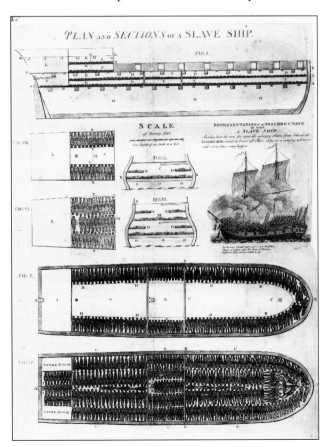

Left: One of several abolitionist prints which were widely distributed during the eighteenth century showing a plan and cross section of a slave ship.

Boston and Salem in Massachusetts, and, to a lesser degree, New York.

The "Triangular Trade"—Myth and Reality

Although for the enslaved Africans the Middle Passage, the terrible voyage from their African homeland to a new and unknown life in the Americas, was the nightmare at the heart of the slave experience, to the slave traders it was merely one crucial phase in a continuing business enterprise that required both luck and commercial judgement to achieve a profitable outcome. Before we look at that Middle Passage we need to consider how the transatlantic slave trade fitted within the wider pattern of international trading links binding together the continents of Europe, Africa, and America. The enduring image of this trade network has been presented by countless history lessons, namely that of the so-called "triangular trade." In the case of Britain, the Netherlands, and France, this involved the slave trader taking a cargo of European goods, mostly poor quality textiles and manufactured items, to the slaving coasts of Africa, exchanging these for a cargo of slaves, tak-

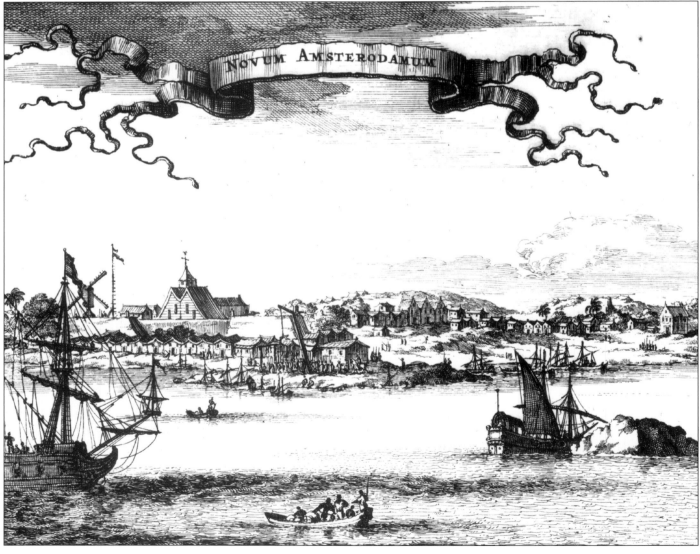

Left: A Puritan Couple. Although states such as Pennsylvania and Rhode Island which were settled by religious nonconformists did not develop economies directly based on slavery, they had less scruples about supplying the slave colonies in the West Indies and their ports supported significant numbers of slavers.

Below left: New Amsterdam Harbor. Among the Dutch colonies established in the seventeenth century, including New Amsterdam, only Surinam on the South American mainland became a large slave-using economy, but the Dutch played a major role in exporting slaves to the Spanish.

Right: Wild Tobacco. Tobacco was a key crop in the slave economies of the British colonies of Virginia and Maryland.

ing these slaves to the Americas where they would be sold in return for a ship's cargo of tropical products, generally sugar or tobacco, and finally returning to the home port in Europe to sell the cargo. The version of the triangular trade operated by North American slavers was somewhat different. They sailed to Africa with a cargo of rum distilled in the colony, exchanged the rum for slaves, transported the slaves to the Caribbean or Brazil where they could be sold in exchange for molasses (made from sugar,) then returned to the home colonies where the molasses was distilled to make more rum. These two neatly structured trade triangles, which might with good fortune yield a high profit on each leg, are said to have financed much of the Industrial Revolution in Britain, as well as paying for the European manufactured goods required by the American colonies.

In fact this account is, as recent scholarship has demonstrated, largely a myth. Like many myths it contains an element of truth but presents a vastly oversimplified picture. The trade between Europe, Africa, and the Americas, as well as shorter trade routes within the Americas themselves, was actually far more complex, with a huge range of routes, products, and trading methods intersecting. Portuguese and Brazilian ships for example, generally sailed a direct route back and forth between Bahia and the African coast, exchanging tobacco for slaves, while other vessels bought slave produced goods, from sugar to precious metals, back to Portugal.

The African trade was certainly an important market for European exports. Each slave voyage, usually financed by a partnership of merchant investors, had to carry a finely judged selection of goods to maximise the number of slaves obtainable. Although some of these goods, including most guns, were of poor quality, in general the evidence suggests that Africans had very definite ideas about the quality and variety of items they required. Slavers who tried to fob them off with inferior goods, or who failed to anticipate changing tastes in items such as luxury cloths

(many of Indian origin,) and Venetian or Dutch beads were frequently left with largely unsaleable cargoes. The precise method by which slaves were bought varied from place to place, but it was normal for gifts to be made to local rulers before trading commenced.

In many places there were shore settlements where slaves were accumulated to await a visiting ship. These varied from substantial forts such as at El Mina, Cape Coast, and elsewhere in the Gold Coast, to rudimentary huts, or in the Niger delta, the rotting hulks of European ships. The death toll among Europeans at these posts or factories as the shore sites were known, was extraordinarily high, with few surviving even for a single year. Slaves being held there, often in dungeons or pens, also suffered an extremely high mortality rate. The captains of visiting ships had to choose whether to cruise along the coast, collecting slaves from a number of sites, including those bought out by canoe a few at a time from less established trading points, or to anchor at a major post until there were sufficient slaves to make a cargo. Both methods could involve a wait of weeks or sometimes months, during which time the crew would also be exposed to a high risk of disease and to slave revolts, which were more common within sight of shore.

Estimates of the speed with which the ship could take on a full cargo of several hundred slaves, together with variations in the ethnic origin favored by buyers in the port of call in the Americas were major factors governing the decision about which African region to select. In a voyage lasting many months without effective communications it was necessary to give the captain considerable discretion, both over where he bought slaves, and over the markets in America or the Caribbean where they were sold. Usually he would be given the right to the proceeds of the sale of ten or so slaves to provide an incentive.

In the West Indies, ships who had sold slaves often used the proceeds to purchase a cargo of sugar or tobacco, but this was by no means always the case. Depending on the state of the harvest when they arrived, and a host of other factors, it was frequently impossible for them to obtain a cargo at a profitable rate. Many returned to Europe loaded only with ballast. Nor was it the case that slave trading was an immensely profitable enterprise. The rate of profit was dependent on a variety of factors, most notably of course, the number of slaves who survived the terrible hardships of the voyage. Certainly a few slaving voyages did produce extraordinarily high returns to their investors of thirty percent or more, but historians who have studied the detailed records of numerous individual traders generally have concluded that returns usually averaged nearer ten percent for Liverpool traders, and between one and six percent for the main French ports. Numerous profitable voyages could be offset by a single uninsurable loss due to insurrection or disease.

Assessing the extent to which the slave trade contributed to the financing of the Industrial Revolution is even more problematic. Scholars have calculated that the direct trade of slavers in ports such as Liverpool and Bristol

contributed only a small fraction of the total economic output of the regions, however, the wider impact of all those involved in financing, insuring, supplying, preparing, and outfitting the slaving fleets, together with the far greater contribution made possible by the systematic expropriation of the products of the slaves' own labor in the West Indies and the mainland colonies of the Americas was undoubtedly a major contributor to European economies at a crucial period.

The Middle Passage

The sheer horror of the conditions endured by millions of Africans in the course of the Middle Passage can easily overwhelm any attempt to describe it. It certainly cannot be mitigated by pointing out that the slavers' crews, and white indentured servants, suffered similar appallingly high mortality rates on transatlantic voyages. Assessments of the relative mortality rates of different routes or different periods, relevant as they no doubt were to slavers' profits, are too abstract to approach the intensity of terror and almost unimaginable cruelties deliberately and routinely imposed in the interests of those profits.

The English abolitionists who in 1788 first published and distributed the notorious print depicting the

Below: The origins of New York—ailing ships and rowing boats share the waters of the Hudson River, with New Amsterdam in the background, 1650.

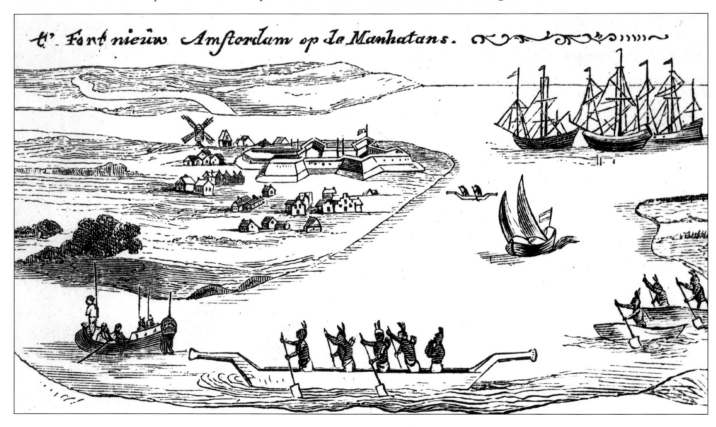

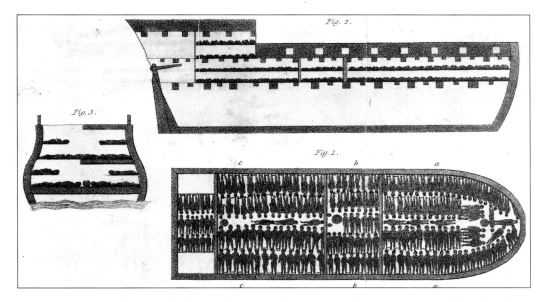

Fig. 2.

Fig. 3.

Fig. 1.

Left: An early nineteenth century print showing the way slaves were packed in below decks on board a slaver.

Below: Stowing the cargo on the slave ship at night.

arrangement of slaves packed together on the Liverpool ship, the *Brookes*, "like books on a shelf" as a contemporary viewer put it, captured the essential basis of the Middle Passage. Nowhere else was the slave society's convenient myth that the slaves were goods not human beings so thoroughly expressed. A witness who sailed on the *Brookes* in 1783 recorded that they packed in over 600 slaves on the 320 ton ship, with over 70 dying on the crossing. Although the majority of slave ships were rather smaller, the deadly confinement was the same. As the ship lay at anchor off the African coast, the carpenter and crew installed the wooden slave decks into the holds that had previously been filled with cargo. Before each purchase the captives were stripped and subjected to a rough and intimate examination by the ship's surgeon in an effort to weed out those already sick. Those selected were often branded with a dealers mark. Once embarked the slaves were slotted on these decks, with only four feet or so of headroom. Men were usually chained in pairs, held at wrist and ankle, while women and children were sometimes allowed to move around the ship by day. All the slaves were usually bought on deck twice daily for an exercise period and forced to perform a shuffling dance under the crew's whips. Food consisted of rice, beans, or yams, palm oil, and a small ration of water. Those who refused to eat or otherwise disobeyed any commands were brutally punished. Slave

An African View of the Middle Passage

Zamba was the son of a slave-trading chief on the Congo River who paid an American captain named Winton to carry him as a passenger to the Americas. On arrival he was tricked and sold into slavery, but he later managed to write an account of his life that was published in England in 1847.

"After many tears and lamentations on both sides, and an assurance on my part that after visiting America and England, I should return with Captain Winton, bringing home as much property as would make me the richest king on the banks of the Congo, I bade adieu to Africa. Little did I then think that I should no more see dear Africa for ever! . . . but when I reflect upon the way in which a merciful providence has acted towards me, I feel my heart swell with gratitude and love. Out of seeming evil, how much good hath fallen to my lot is not to be reckoned. The Almighty . . . hath since repaid me with that inestimable treasure, which is from heaven . . . which will never perish, or rust, not fade away.

"Captain Winton accommodated me with a handsome state-room and we left the Congo on the first day of October 1800. I found that, including my own thirty-two, there were in all four hundred and twenty-two slaves on board: but as the vessel was of 500 tons burthen, they were not so crowded for space as I have since learned has often been the case with emigrants from Europe to America; their accommodation, however was miserable. The ship's lower deck was divided fore and aft into compartments of about six and into each of these divisions four slaves were put; to lie down, or sit, or take it as they chose. The planks were intended to keep them from rolling when the sea was rough. Of course, they had nothing but the hard deck to lie upon. In regard to clothing they were very scantily supplied: in general, both male and female had a yard and a half; or two yards of Osnaburghs wrapped round their loins; and some of them had a piece of cloth, or a handkerchief; bound round their heads. The males were all linked two and two by small chain round the ankle. As for provision, they were much better off than in the generality of slave-ships; and this, strange as it may appear, they owed to the avarice rather than the humanity of the captain. The motives of the latter, however, were of little moment to the poor slaves, provided the end was for their advantage. The slaves were supplied for breakfast with a fair ration of ground Indian corn boiled, with a spoonful of molasses to each; they generally had boiled rice for dinner; and supper they received each about half a pound of ship biscuit, with a little morsel of beef or pork; too much of this latter would, no doubt, have created thirst. Although this captain (as will be shown in the sequel of my narrative) acted in a most dishonourable and treacherous manner towards me, and was totally devoid of all Christian principle, yet, to serve his own ends in the matter of the slaves, he acted the part of a humane and considerate man. He told me, in the course of our voyage, that, in the early part of his experience in the slave-trade, he had seen as many slaves as he had with him at present shipped on board a vessel of 200 tons, where they were literally packed on the top of each other; and, consequently, from ill air, confinement, and scanty or unwholesome provision, disease was generated to such an extent that in several cases had known only one-half survive to the end of the voyage; and these, as he termed it, in a very unmarketable condition. He found, therefore, that, by allowing them what he called sufficient room and good provisions, with kind treatment, his speculations turned out much better in regard to the amount of dollars received; and that was all he cared for.

"For the first few days, the most of us—I mean the blacks—were laid down with seasickness: but, the weather being fine, that was soon got over. The captain caused the hatches to be kept open night and day (except only upon two occasions) during the whole voyage; and after daylight set in he allowed about one-fourth of his cargo to come on deck for two hours by rotation. He had always four of his men with loaded muskets and fixed bayonets, day and night on deck; but during this trip there never was the slightest attempt at rioting and mutiny. The only misfortune that befell us was this: after being about 15 days out to sea, one evening, about sunset—the ship with all sail set, going down the trades at the rate of five knots an hour—in the clap of the hand, or at least more suddenly than a stranger to these latitudes could imagine, a heavy squall struck the ship, carrying away great part of the loftier spars and sails, and laying her very nearly on her beam ends. In a few minutes a tremendous sea rose, and although the squall blew over in about a quarter of an hour, and the ship regained her position' the poor slaves below, altogether unprepared for such an occurrence, were mostly thrown on the lee-side, where they lay heaped on the top of each other; their fetters rendered many of them helpless, and before they could be arranged in their proper places, and relieved from their pressure on each other, it was found that 15 of them were smothered or crushed to death, besides a great number who were cruelly bruised. The Captain seemed considerably vexed; but the only (or at least the chief) grievance to him was the sudden loss of some five or six thousand dollars."

Right: A Kongo warrior in ceremonial attire.

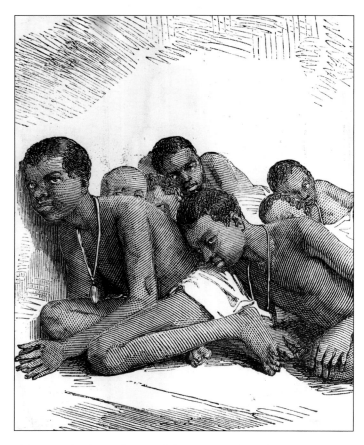

Left: The sitting position of slaves packed on a slaver. In the Middle Passage male slaves spent almost all their time chained below decks to prevent revolts.

Right: A print depicting slavers inspecting chained captives prior to buying them from African merchants. In the foreground are some of the trade goods, cloth, firearms, and bottles of gin.

ships stocked crude metal braces used to force open the mouth so that food could be forced down the throat. Although some captains forbade the crew from interfering with the women, there was a constant danger of rape. Recalcitrant slaves were whipped, clubbed, or simply cast overboard. A constant watch was kept to prevent suicide or rebellion, with savage reprisals following unsuccessful attempts. After a revolt on the American ship *Kentucky* in 1844, 46 men and one woman were hanged, mutilated while still alive, then shot and thrown into the sea.

In bad weather the Africans could be confined in the badly ventilated holds for weeks. Falconbridge, a surgeon on slave ships who left a journal of his experiences, published in 1788, wrote of the inevitable consequences:

"fluxes and fevers among the Negroes ensued. The deck, was so covered with the blood and mucus which had proceeded from them in consequence of the flux that it resembled a slaughterhouse . . . Numbers of the slaves having fainted, they were carried on deck where several of them died and the rest with great difficulty were restored."

It is likely that the traumatic impact of the experience itself killed many, a cause contemporary observers recognized as "melancholy" from which many never recovered. Dysentery, known as "flux" was a major killer, as were

yaws, scurvy, smallpox, measles, and "fever." Opthalmia was also a regular problem—on the French ship *Le Rodeur* in 1819, thirty-nine slaves who went blind were simply thrown overboard. The barely trained doctors that slave ships carried in an effort to minimize the economic cost of these outbreaks seldom made any significant difference.

As might be expected, the longer the slaves were kept in such appalling conditions the higher the rate of attrition. The proportion of people who died on individual voyages varied between a low of around two or three percent to upwards of twenty-five out of every hundred. Shipwrecks could exact an even higher toll—in 1737 only sixteen slaves out of 716 survived the wreck of the Dutch ship *Leusden*. Also, large numbers weakened by the journey died while awaiting sale in the ports of the Americas. In Jamaica it was estimated that between 1655 and 1737, of the 676,276 slaves recorded on arrival, 31,181 died while

Right and Far right: The fort at El Mina in Ghana, founded by the Portuguese as São Jorge da Mina in 1482, to exploit the gold of the region. Later it became a major base for the export of slaves by the British.

Slaves in Mutiny

In a book published in 1734 a slaver, William Snelgrave, published this account of slave mutinies on board ship:

". . . these Mutinies are generally occasioned by the sailors ill usage of these poor people, when on board the Ship wherein they are transported to our Plantations . . .

"The first Mutiny I saw among the Negroes, happened during my first Voyage, in the Year 1704. It was on board the "Eagle Galley" of London, commanded by my Father, with whom I was as Purser. We had bought our Negroes in the River of Old Callabar in the Bay of Guinea. At the time of their mutinying we were in that River, having four hundred of them on board, and not above ten white men who were able to do Service; For several of our Ship's Company were dead, and many more sick; besides, two of our Boats were just then gone with twelve people on Shore to fetch Wood, which lay in sight of the Ship. All these Circumstances put the Negroes on consulting how to mutiny, which they did at four a clock in the Afternoon, just as they went to Supper. but as we had always carefully examined the mens Irons, both Morning and Evening, none had got them off; which in a great measure contributed to our Preservation. Three white men stood on the Watch with Cutlaces in their hands. One of them was on the forecastle, a stout fellow, seeing some of the Men Negroes take hold of the chief mate, in order to throw him over board, he laid on them so heartily with the flat side of his Cutlace, that they soon quitted the mate, who escaped from them, and run on the Quarter Deck to get Arms. I was then sick with an Ague, and lying on a Couch in the great Cabbin, the fit being just come on. However, I no sooner heard the Outcry, that the Slaves were mutinying, but I took two Pistols, and run on the Deck with them; where meeting with my Father and the chief Mate, I delivered a Pistol to each of them. Whereupon they went forward on the Booms, calling to the Nergoe Men that were on the Forecastle; but they did not regard their Threats, being busy with the Centry, (who had disengaged the chief Mate), and they would have certainly killed him

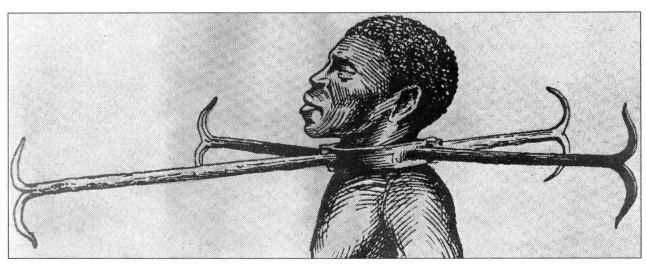

with his own Cutlace, could they have got it from him; but they could not break the Line Wherewith the handle was fastened to his Wrist. And so, tho' they had seized him, yet they could not make use of his Cutlace. Being thus disappointed, they endeavoured to throw him overboard, but he held so fast by one of them that they could not do it. My Father seeing this stout Man in so much Danger, ventured amongst the negroes to save him; and fired his Pistol over their Heads, thinking to frighten them. But a lusty Slave struck him with a Billet so hard, that he was almost stunned. The Slave was going to repeat his Blow, when a young Lad about seventeen years old, whom we had been kind to, interposed his Arm, and received the Blow, by which his Arm-bone was fractured. At the same instant the Mate fired his Pistol, and shot the Negroe that had struck my Father. At the sight of this the Mutiny ceased, and all the Men-negroes on the Forecastle threw themselves flat on their Faces, crying out for Mercy . . .

"On another occasion, talking with Captain Messery of the Ferrers and understanding from him, that he had never been on the Coast of Guinea before, I took the liberty to observe to him, 'That as he had on board so many Negroes of one Town and language, it required the utmost Care and Management to keep them form mutinying . . .'

"This he took kindly, and having asked my Advice about other matters, took his leave, inviting me to come next day to see him. I went accordingly on board his Ship, about three a clock in the afternoon. At four a clock the Negroes went to Supper, and Captain Messery desired me to excuse him for a quarter of an hour, whilst he went forward to see the Men-Negroes served with Victuals. I observed from the Quarter-Deck, that he himself put Pepper and Palm Oil amongst the Rice they were going to eat. When he came back to me, I could not forbear observing to him, 'How imprudent it was in him to do so: For tho' it was proper for a Commander sometimes to go forward, and observe how things were managed; yet he ought to take a proper time, and

have a good many of his white People in Arms when he went; or else the having him so much in their Power, might encourage the slaves to mutiny: For he might depend upon it, they always aim at the chief Person in the Ship, whom they soon distinguish by the respect shown him by the rest of the People.' . . .

"He sailed three days after for Jamaica. Some Months after I went to that place, where at my arrival I found his Ship, and had the following melancholy account of his Death, which happened about ten days after he left the Coast of Guinea.

"Being on the Forecastle of the Ship, amongst the Men-negroes, when they were eating their Victuals, they laid hold on him, and beat out his Brains with the little Tubs, out of which they eat their boiled Rice. This Mutiny having been plotted amongst all the grown negroes on board, they run to the forepart of the Ship in a body, and endeavoured to force the Barricado on the Quarter-Deck, not regarding the Musquets or Half Pikes, that were presented to their Breasts by the white Men through the Loopholes. So that at last the chief mate was obliged to order one of the Quarter-deck Guns laden with Partridge-Shot, to be fired amongst them; which occasioned a terrible Destruction: For there were near eight Negroes kill'd and drowned, many jumping overboard when the Gun was fired. This indeed put an end to the Mutiny, but most of the Slaves that remained alive grew so sullen, that several of them were starved to death, obstinately refusing to take any sustenance."

Left: A neck ring used as a punishment in the West Indies prevented a slave from lying down.

Right: A Virginia slave auction; a dealer inspecting slaves prior to purchase.

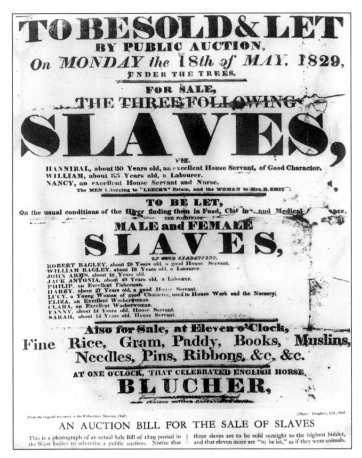

TO BE SOLD & LET
BY PUBLIC AUCTION,
On MONDAY the 18th of MAY, 1829,
UNDER THE TREES.
FOR SALE,
THE THREE FOLLOWING

SLAVES,

VIZ.

HANNIBAL, about 30 Years old, an excellent House Servant, of Good Character.
WILLIAM, about 35 Years old, a Labourer.
NANCY, an excellent House Servant and Nurse.
The MEN belonging to "LEECH'S" Estate, and the WOMAN to Mrs. D. SMIT?

TO BE LET,
On the usual conditions of the Hirer finding them in Food, Clothing and Medical attendance,
THE FOLLOWING
MALE and FEMALE

SLAVES,

OF GOOD CHARACTERS,

ROBERT BAGLEY, about 20 Years old, a good House Servant.
WILLIAM BAGLEY, about 18 Years old, a Labourer.
JOHN ARMS, about 18 Years old.
JACK ANTONIA, about 40 Years old, a Labourer.
HARRY, about 27 Years old, a good House Servant.
PHILIP, an Excellent Fisherman.
LUCY, a Young Woman of good Character, used to House Work and the Nursery;
ELIZA, an Excellent Washerwoman.
CLARA, an Excellent Washerwoman.
FANNY, about 14 Years old, House Servant.
SARAH, about 14 Years old, House Servant.

Also for Sale, at Eleven o'Clock,
Fine Rice, Gram, Paddy, Books, Muslins, Needles, Pins, Ribbons, &c. &c.
AT ONE O'CLOCK, THAT CELEBRATED ENGLISH HORSE,

BLUCHER,

From the original document in the Wilberforce Museum, Hull
[Photo : Doughtys, Ltd., Hull]

AN AUCTION BILL FOR THE SALE OF SLAVES

This is a photograph of an actual Sale Bill of 1829 posted in the West Indies to advertise a public auction. Notice that three slaves are to be sold outright to the highest bidder, and that eleven more are "to be let," as if they were animals.

Left: A poster advertising a slave sale.

Sugar was the key to the huge numbers of slaves imported into Brazil and the Caribbean islands in the seventeenth and eighteenth centuries. As we have seen, the growing of sugar using slave plantations on the Atlantic islands provided the impetus behind the early years of Portuguese involvement in the slave trade, and it was also crucial to the development of their vast colony in Brazil. However, it was the Dutch merchants, taking advantage of the experience gained during their brief occupation of Brazil, and in their colony of Surinam, who were primarily responsible for spreading intensive sugar cultivation to the Caribbean. Barbados, and on a lesser scale Jamaica, were the major British-controlled sugar-growing regions, Saint-Domingue the main French colony, and Cuba, coming into the trade rather later, the main Spanish source, together with the numerous lesser islands of the West Indies.

The effect of the switch to sugar cultivation on the flow of slaves, and on the wealth of the planters, was immediate. In the 1640s as many as a hundred ship loads of slaves and indentured servants were landed at Barbados each year, while in the French Caribbean islands as a whole, the total number of slaves imported leapt from a tiny 2,500 in the period from 1625 to 1650, to 28,800 in the following 25 years. Between 1640 and 1700, 85,100 Africans were landed in Jamaica and an almost incredible 134,500 on the small island of Barbados. Even these figures were dwarfed by those for the eighteenth century. Sugar production boomed, stimulated by growing European demand which was promoted by planters' interests. Field slaves on sugar plantations labored in the planting and cutting seasons from sunrise to sunset, with perhaps a break at midday if work was on schedule. One of many contemporary accounts described the scene:

"There were about a hundred men and women of different ages . . . the majority of them naked or covered with rags. The sun shone down with full force on their heads. Sweat rolled from all parts of their bodies . . . Exhaustion

still in the harbor. Other unfortunates did not survive much longer—one captain reported to his ship owners that their credit in the Indies could be harmed considerably as so many of their "parcels" had expired within twenty-four hours of sale.

African Slaves in the Americas

On arrival in the Americas surviving slaves were prepared for sale. Palm oil was used to make their skin brighter, while wounds and scars were concealed as well as possible. Often this was the final task of the ship's surgeon. Those who were clearly too sick to be passed off as fit were sold separately. Merchants sometimes bought them cheaply as a speculation, hoping to profit from reselling those who recovered. The public auction was the standard method of sale, though private arrangements made through the local agent of the slave trader were also possible. In Spanish colonies there was an elaborate bureaucratic tax collecting procedure, involving measuring and recording details of each slave and branding them again on the breast with the royal mark, in the form of the letter R surmounted by a crown. Since in most areas there were never enough slaves imported to meet the colonists' continuing demands bidding was usually brisk and the prices paid for healthy men and women rose steadily. On occasions the terrified slaves were seized by their would-be purchasers in a brutal rush for the most promising imports, known as a "scramble."

Above right: A contemporary illustration of a slave auction in Virginia captures a sense of what, for the white bidders, had become a routine part of business life attracting little attention. For the black family on the block however, sale to new masters could herald permanent separation.

Right: A New Orleans slave sale. The threat of being sold, with the consequent break-up of families and forced transfer to new and unfamiliar circumstances, was among the main sources of anger and grief in African-American communities throughout the slave-holding states of the South.

SLAVES FOR SALE : A SCENE IN NEW ORLEANS

Profit and Loss

Bryan Edwards (1743-1800,) an absentee planter, gave this view of the profits of a Jamaican sugar plantation in the eighteenth century:

"A sugar plantation consists of three great parts; the Lands, the Buildings, and the Stock: but before I proceed to discriminate their relative proportions and value, it may be proper to observe, that the business of sugar planting is the sort of adventure in which the man that engages, must engage deeply. There is no medium, and very seldom the possibility of retreat. A British country gentleman, who is content to jog on without risk, on the moderate profits of his own moderate farm, will startle to hear that it requires a capital of no less than 30,000 pounds sterling to embark in this employment with a fair prospect of advantage . . .

"As therefore, a plantation yielding, on an average, 200 hogsheads of sugar annually, requires, as I conceive, not less than 300 acres to be planted in canes, the whole extent of such a property must be reckoned at 900 acres. I am persuaded that the sugar plantations in Jamaica making those returns,

commonly exceed, rather than fall short of; this estimate; not as hath been ignorantly asserted, from a fond and avaricious propensity in the proprietors to engross more land than is necessary; but because, from the nature of the soil, and rugged surface of the country, the lands vary greatly in quality, and it is seldom that even 300 acres of soil in contiguity, fit for the production of sugar, can be procured . . .

"The stock on a plantation of the magnitude described, cannot prudently consist of less than 250 Negroes, 80 steers and 60 mules . . . The cost of the stock, therefore, may be stated as follows:

Jamaican Currency

250 Negroes, at £70 each	17,500
80 steers, at £15	1,300
60 mules, at £28	1,680
Total in currency equal to	£14,557 sterling
	£20,380

Let us now bring the whole into one point of view

Lands	14,100
Buildings	7,000
Stock	20, 380
Total in currency	£41,480

Which is only £520 short of £42,000 Jamaica currency, or £30,000 sterling, the sum first mentioned.

Left: Punishment of slaves on a plantation in Surinam. Under constant threat from rebellions and attacks by the large communities of Maroons, or escaped slaves, living in the forested interior, the planters in the Dutch colony became notorious for the brutality of their treatment of slaves and the harshness of plantation conditions.

"The produce of such a plantation Sterling.

300 Hogshead of sugar, at £15 sterling per hogshead

               3,000

130 puncheons of rum, at £10 sterling per puncheon

               1,300

Gross returns   £4,300

"But the reader is not to imagine that all this, or even the sugar alone, is so much clear profit. The annual disbursements are first to be deducted, and very heavy they are; nor is any opinion more erroneous than that which supposes they are provided for by the rum.

Annual Supplies from Great Britain & Ireland.

1st Negro Clothing; viz

1,500 yards of Osnaburgh cloth, or German linen.

650 yards of blue bays, or pennistones, for a warm frock for each Negro.

350 yards of striped linesys for the women

250 yards of coarse check for shirts for the boilers, tradesmen, domestics, and the children.

3 dozen of coarse blankets for lying-in women, and sick Negroes. 18 dozen of coarse hats.

2nd Tools

For the carpenters and coopers, to the amount of £25 sterling, including 2 or 3 dozen of falling axes.

3rd Miscellaneous articles

To the sum of £850 sterling. To the sum are to be added the following very heavy charges within the Island; viz.

	Jamaican Currency
Overseer's or manager's salary	200
Distiller's ditto	70
Two other white servants, £60 each	120
A white carpenter's wages	100
Maintenance of five white servants exclusive of their allowance of salted provisions, £40 each	200

Medical care of the Negroes (at 6s per annum for each Negro) and extra cases, which are paid for separately	100
Millwright's coppersmith's plumber's, and smith's bills, annually	250
colonial taxes, public and parochial	200
Annual supply of mules and steers	300
Wharfage and storage of goods land and shipped	100
American staves and heading, for hogsheads and puncheons	150
A variety of small occasional supplies of different kinds, supposed	50
Equal to £1,300 sterling; being in currency £1,840	

"The total amount, therefore, of the annual contingent charges of all kinds, is £2,150 sterling, which is precisely one-half the gross returns; leaving the other moiety, or £2,150 sterling, and no more, clear profit to the planter, being seven per cent on his capital . . .

"With these and other drawbacks (to say nothing of the devastations which are sometimes occasioned by fires and hurricanes, destroying in a few hours the labour of years) it is not wonderful that the profits should frequently dwindle to nothing; or rather that a sugar estate, with all its boasted advantages, should sometimes prove a millstone about the neck of its unfortunate proprietor."

Right: An early representation of sugar cane and the making of sugar in the Caribbean.

was stamped on every face . . . The pitiless eye of the Manager patrolled the gang and several foremen armed with long whips moved periodically between them, giving stinging blows to all who, worn out by fatigue, were compelled to take a rest, men or women, young or old."

For those slaves who had the highly valued skills and experience of distillers and boilers necessary to refine the sugar, or the subsidiary skills such as carpentry and metal-work necessary to maintain the plantation estates, the immediate demands of labor could be somewhat easier, as they were for the house servants (although these posts, too, held hardships and dangers). For the field hands, who formed the majority of the plantation labor force, however, life was brutal and short. It has been estimated that, in the Caribbean as a whole, one in three newly imported Africans died within three years of arrival, while in Barbados between 1764 and 1771 around 35,000 slaves were imported but the total population grew by only 5,000. Planters worked on the assumption that they would have to replace at least five percent of their labor force annually. The ratio of men to women in these slave societies varied, with Barbados, for example, having a much higher percentage of women, and hence a larger locally-born Creole slave population than on the other islands. In all of them, however, the conditions were such that, until abolition, in contrast to the situation on the North American mainland, there was no prospect of the African population reproducing, and a large influx of new slaves was needed each year to maintain the existing numbers.

Both the local legal systems and the impromptu punishments administered by planters and their overseers were based on the regular use of the most brutal of corporal punishments. Legal codes, whether the planter-defined laws of the British Caribbean or the ostensibly less restrictive *Côde Noir* imposed in the French, prescribed a series of brutal punishments, including, as one eighteenth century account noted, "of slitting the Nose, branding in the Forehead with hot Iron, cutting off the Ears, and in some Islands, even that of taking off a Limb." More common though were the everyday brutalities of severe floggings and beatings often administered even to heavily pregnant women and to quite young children. Privileged slaves could be punished simply by reducing them to the ranks of field hands. The historian John Thornton recorded the case of two favored Brazilian domestic slaves, named Ines and Juliana, who in 1613 in Bahia made the mistake of testifying against their master to the Inquisition. He had them transferred to his sugar estate and both died within a short time, the victims of repeated whippings.

The sexual exploitation of slave women was taken for granted in the plantation colonies of the West Indies and throughout South America. As the historian of Brazilian slavery, Gilberto Freyre, noted in his epic work *The Masters and the Slaves*, the sons of Brazilian slaveholders in the estate big houses were positively encouraged to exercise their "precocious depravity" with the slave women. In the Caribbean, planters and their overseers often set up house more or less openly with their favorite among the slaves. Thomas Thistlewood, an overseer in Jamaica in the mid-eighteenth century, kept unusually frank diaries in which he recorded the details of his sexual activities and the rewards he gave to the slave women involved. He

Right: Slaves for sale at a dealer in Brazil. This print from a traveler's journal illustrates the pitiful and emaciated condition of many Africans who survived the horrors of the Middle Passage.

Slaves in Rebellion

"Tacky's Rebellion," in 1760 was the most bloody of the numerous small revolts in the British colonies of the Caribbean. Here, it is described by the planter Bryan Edwards:

"Having collected themselves into a body about one o'clock in the morning, they proceeded to the fort at Port Maria, killed the sentinel, and provided themselves with as great a quantity of arms and ammunition as this they could conveniently dispose of. Being by this time joined by a number of their countrymen from the neighbouring plantations, they marched up the high road that led to the interior parts of the country, carrying death and desolation as they went. At Ballard's about four in the morning, in which finding every one of them in the most savage manner, and literally drank their blood mixed with rum. At Esher, and other estates, they exhibited the same tragedy; and then set fire to the buildings and canes. In one morning they murdered between thirty and forty Whites and Mulattoes, not sparing even infants at the breast, before their progress was stopped. Tacky, the Chief; was killed in the woods by one of the parties that went in pursuit of them; but some others of the ring-leaders being taken, and a general inclination to revolt appearing among all the Koromantyn Negroes in the island, it was thought necessary to make a few terrible examples of some of the most guilty. Of three who were clearly proved to have been concerned in the murders committed at Ballard's Valley, one was condemned to be burnt, and the other two to be hung up alive in irons, and left to perish in that dreadful situation. The wretch that was burnt, was made to sit on the ground, and his body, being chained to an iron stake, the fire was applied to his feet. he uttered not a groan, and saw his legs reduced to ashes with the utmost firmness and composure; after which, one of his arms by some means getting loose, he snatched a brand from the fire that was consuming him, and flung it in the face of the executioner. the two that were hung up alive were indulged, at their own request, with a hearty meal immediately before they were suspended on the gibbet, which was erected in the parade of the town of Kingston. From that time, until they expired, they never uttered the least complaint, except only of cold in the night, but diverted themselves all the day long in discourse with their countrymen, who were permitted, very improperly, to surround the gibbet. On the seventh day a notion prevailed among the spectators, that one of them wished to communicate an important secret to his master, my near relation; who being in St Mary's parish, the commanding officer sent for me. I endeavoured, by means of an interpreter, to let him know that I was present; but I could not understand what he said in return. I remember that both he and his fellow-sufferer laughed immoderately at something that occurred, I know not what. The next morning one of them silently expired, as did the other on the . . . ninth day."

Above: A bound slave being beaten on a plantation in Brazil.

Below: An eighteenth century print depicting both Europeans and African slaves at work in the processing of tobacco.

noted for example gifts to a woman named Jenny of "2 yards of Brown Oznabrig, 4 bitts, 4 yards of striped holland, 8 bitts, etc." while his favorite, Phibbah, apparently accumulated sufficient money to give him a gift of a gold ring when they finally parted after many years. Sexual contacts ranged from assaults and rapes to ostensibly voluntary contacts over extended periods, during which, if the evidence (which comes almost exclusively from the white men) is to be believed, real affection developed. Women were on many occasions able to use these relationships to secure both material advantages and even freedom for themselves and any resulting children. In a very few instances slave owners even married their slaves—eight such marriages were recorded in Martinique in 1660. Far more commonly, though, slave women and girls were vulnerable to the transitory lusts of their masters and overseers. Inquisition records from Catholic colonies also reveal sporadic evidence of homosexual exploitation, as does Freyre in his Brazilian history. Inevitably these contacts, and relationships between slaves and white women, are far less well documented but undoubtedly took place.

Slave Economies and Slave Societies

Although the plantations and mines of Brazil, which imported a vast total of over four million slaves, and the various plantation colonies of the Caribbean, whose total imports amounted to between four and five million, accounted for a substantial majority of the total slave

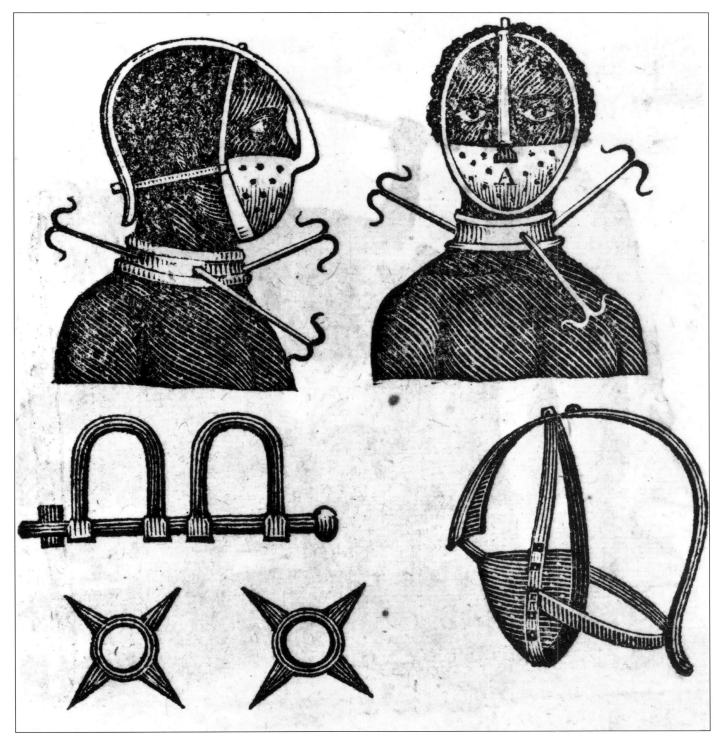

Above: The inhumane treatment of slaves—a variety of devices used to punish disobedient slaves.

shipments, a further one and a half million or so were destined for Spanish America. Mexico imported large numbers of slaves through the ports of Cartegena and Vera Cruz, especially in the early decades of the seventeenth century, although high mortality rates meant that the overall slave population remained very small. A total of about 100,000 Africans were imported into Peru after a further difficult journey across Panama and by ship to Lima. Slaves worked as domestic servants, as craftsmen in towns, in small-scale agriculture, and in neighboring Bolivia alongside Native Americans in the famous silver mines at Potosi.

A similar total number was shipped into the port of Buenos Aires and from there to various regions in present-day Argentina and Uruguay, with far smaller numbers traveling overland to Chile. Both gold mining and plantation agriculture required the importation of around 250,000 slaves into Columbia, while cocoa growing accounted for most of the 120,000 or so in Venezuela.

Variations in the working conditions of Africans in the

different economic and social contexts to which they were forcibly transplanted in the Americas had a far reaching impact on the nature and extent of the community life that they were able to develop. Scholars now see these variations in conditions in the Americas as far more important in the development of African-American cultures than older theories that argued that the trauma of the Middle Passage and the subsequent mixing of ethnic groups in the plantations had erased all possibilities of cultural continuities with Africa.

The work of anthropologists such as Melville and Frances Herskovits and, more recently, of the art historian Robert Farris Thompson has made it clear that there are indeed a wide range of African derived cultural features throughout the Americas, but that the extent to which they have survived, evolved, and adapted depends to a large degree on the circumstances of community life both during slavery and since abolition. In particular a contrast has been drawn between plantation colonies in the American South and those of the Caribbean and Brazil. In the former, as we shall see in the following chapter, paternalist doctrine and economic interest combined to intertwine closely the life of the slaves with that of the masters. In most Caribbean and Brazilian plantations, despite the brutal treatment and intensive labor with the resulting high-death toll and low fertility rates, slaves living in separate villages on each plantation were able to develop relatively greater areas of effective community life. This was primarily due to their reliance on the individual plots allocated to each slave from which he or she was expected to produce

Above: A number of slave marriages in a rich Brazilian house. As elsewhere, house slaves could often accumulate considerable finery and the celebration of slave weddings was marked by festivities. In general, though, the unions formed lacked legal standing and families could be broken up on the whims of the master.

Right: The town and bay of Port Royal, the metropolis of the Island of Martinique, one of the more important of the French slave colonies in the West Indies.

the bulk of the crops necessary for sustenance. Slaves were expected to work these plots in addition to their labor in the sugar fields, but were given time in the evenings and on Sundays to do so. The surplus output of these plots, on which planters often remarked bitterly that the slaves worked with far greater energy and efficiency than during their enforced labor, were the basis of a thriving market economy throughout the Caribbean. Other spare time was used by those who had a skill to sell or could make craft goods to add to their income. Slave women in particular were allowed to travel off the plantation on Sundays to attend the bustling markets, providing an arena of independence in which they could accumulate a modest material wealth and interact with free blacks and other slaves. In Jamaica it has been calculated that by 1774 slaves owned twenty percent of all circulating cash. Although planters were often unhappy about the degree of economic independence achieved by slaves and free blacks, the more realistic had to recognize that the economies of these societies were actually dependent on this thriving trade.

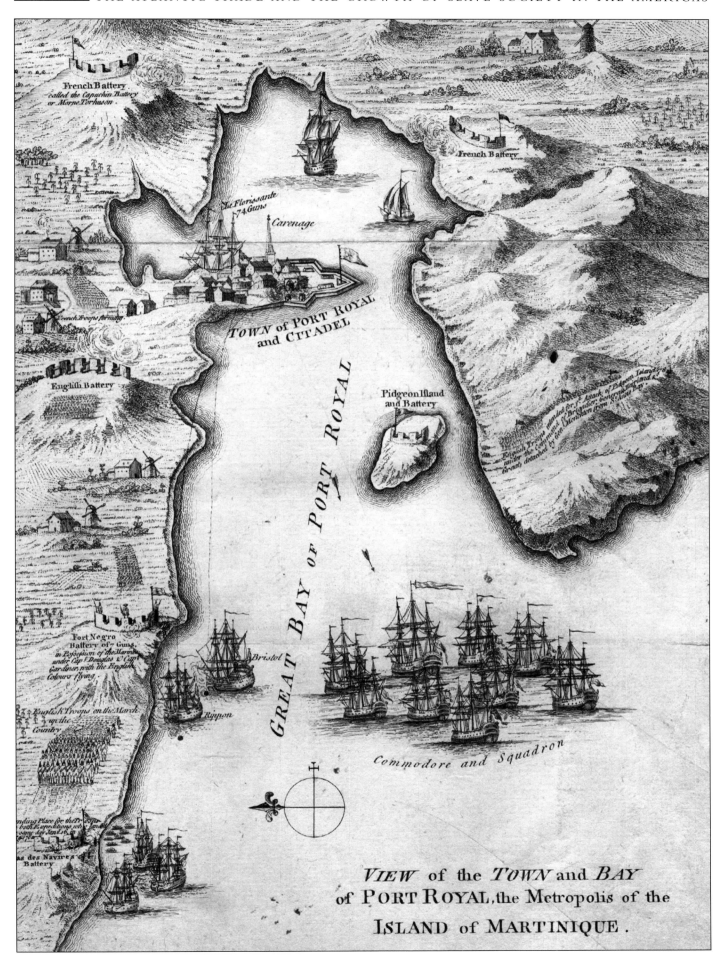

French Battery called the Capuchin Battery or Morne Torbuson.

French Battery

The Florissante 74 Guns

Carenage

TOWN of PORT ROYAL and CITADEL

French Troops forming

English Battery

Pidgeon Island and Battery

English Troops intended for 1st Attack of Pidgeon Island &c under the Command of Brigadier General England &c Grant, detached by Gen. Monckton from St Ann's Bay

GREAT BAY of PORT ROYAL

Fort Negro Battery of 7 Guns, in Possession of the Marines under Cap.t Douglas & Capt. Gardener with the English Colours flying.

Bristol

Rippon

English Troops on the March up the Country

Commodore and Squadron

Landing Place for the Troops of both Expeditions

des Navires Battery

VIEW of the TOWN and BAY
of PORT ROYAL, the Metropolis of the
ISLAND of MARTINIQUE.

The planters themselves fed on cattle and poultry, fruit and vegetables, raised on the slave gardens and purchased by their domestic servants at the Sunday markets. In the towns of Spanish America and Brazil slaves with skills, such as blacksmiths, and petty traders, were often allowed to work independently on a full time basis, passing on a proportion of their incomes to their masters. Alongside this relatively independent economic activity, in many communities of the French and Spanish Caribbean and Latin America African-Americans were able to use Catholicism as a mask behind which they could develop largely African-derived new religions such as *Candomble* and *Santeria*.

The ultimate expression of independent activity by Africans in the slave societies of the Americas was the possibility of rebellion or of escape. Haiti provides the only example of a successful rebellion, in which slaves under the leadership of Toussaint l'Ouverture overthrew their masters in a bloody uprising before fending off both French efforts at reconquest and a large invasion force sent by the British. The unique conditions which allowed this remarkable achievement arose from the impact of intellectual and social instability promoted by the French Revolution in a society with a huge number of recently imported Africans. Between 1785 and 1790 over 30,000 new slaves were imported each year to work in the harsh conditions of the island's sugar and coffee plantations. A substantial community of around 40,000 white colonists was fragmented as divisions between rich landowners and poor whites mirrored those in France, while some 30,000 free blacks

known as mulattos, including wealthy planters, were subject to humiliating legal and social restrictions. Vastly outnumbering both were the 500,000 slaves.

White alarm at the direction of developments in Paris prompted increasing restrictions on the mulatto population and the harsh suppression of an attempted uprising in 1790. Rumors abounded that the emancipation of all slaves was imminent. With local politics in turmoil, a huge slave revolt erupted in August 1791. By late September over a thousand plantations had been burned and many hundreds of whites killed, with many more blacks indiscriminately murdered in reprisals. The reactionary policies of the white landowners alienated many important mulattos who had initially opposed the slave rebels in pursuit of their own interests. However, by late 1792 the arrival of 6,000 French troops had briefly stabilized the situation, although significant areas remained in rebel hands. Under the direction of the radical officials sent from France, pro-Royalist whites were forcibly displaced across the country by military bands of free mulattos.

In 1793, the outbreak of war with Spain and England led both the Republican administration and the Spanish to arm black rebels as mercenaries. Facing an English invasion the desperate regime declared all slavery abolished on August 29, 1793. Arms flowed to the blacks who fought for all sides. The genius of Toussaint l'Ouverture, who was a low-ranking freed slave, on the eve of the revolution, was in forging a united black military force from the turmoil and conflicting loyalties of the years of war that ensued. The

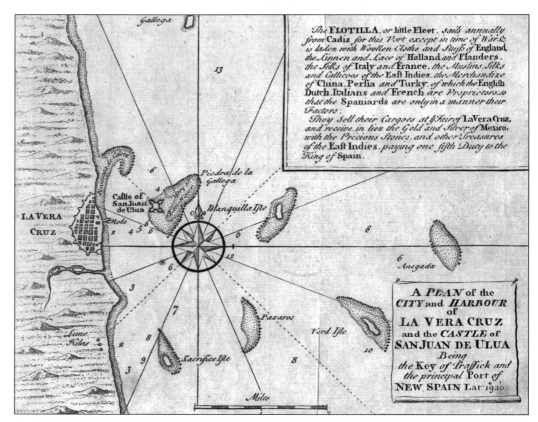

Right: A plan of the city and harbor of La Vera Cruz—the principal port of New Spain and a major transit point for slaves destined for the Spanish colonies in South America.

Goddard wife of Doctor John Hicks Goddard a mulatto Woman Slave named Orian with her future issue and increase hereafter to be born, also two Negro boy Slaves named Edmond and Tom James to her and her heirs forever Item. I give and bequeath unto my daughter Judith Ann Cox a Negro Woman Slave named Mary with her future Issue and Increase hereafter to be born to her and her heirs forever. Item. I give and bequeath unto my Son Wiltshire Rider Cox a negro boy Slave named Sargeant to him and his heirs forever. Item. I give and bequeath unto my Son Samuel Brandford Cox a Negro boy Slave named Cullymore to him and his heirs forever. Lastly all the rest residue and remainder of my Estate both real and personal of every nature kind and quality whatsoever I give and bequeath unto my Sons and Daughters in this my Will named equally to be divided between them share and share alike and their heirs forever. And I do hereby nominate and appoint my said Son in Law John Hicks Goddard and my said Son John Williams Cox Executors of this my said Will hereby revoking all former and other Will or Wills by me at any time heretofore made, and I do declare this only my last Will and Testament. In Witness whereof I have hereunto set my hand and seal this twentieth day of February One thousand seven

71

Right: List of persons
manumitted in Jamaica,
1822.

115

Date of Manumission	Name of the person manumitted	Consideration money paid or otherwise	By whom
1822 March 6	Charlotte Cadogan Grant al Matilda	£140	Francis Smith
1821 Sept.r 10	John William Rees	10/	Ann Rees
Aug.t 29	Adelaide	£100	Amand Reinouard
Dec.r 12	George al George Spencer	10/	Isaac Marache De Leon
1822 March 14	Mark Shroud	none	Commissioners of H.M. Navy Rich.d Croasdaile
1821 Nov.r 16	Mary al Mary Menzies	None	Johanna Menzies & al Trus
June 13	Eliza White	£1 each	Kosciusco Ferrell &ux & al
1820 Jan.y 13	Hope al Grace Williams	None	Dorothy Williams
1822 Feb.y 20	Mary Ann Eliza Jones	£10	Isabella Fishley
March 13 {	Elizabeth Walters / Ann Walters	£100	Thomas Lewis Warren
1821 Dec.r 3	Mary Roberts	10/	Christian McKenley
1822 March 26	Nancy Wallace	£100	Ex.t of Jacob Bassan
March 23	Amelia	10/	Dorothy Cumming
Feb.y 26	John Lewis	none	John Lewis
March 22	Rich.d Alex.r Aldred	none	Eliz.th Ann Aldred
1821 Nov.r 22 {	Jane al Jane Anderson & Chi.d / Elizabeth Fleming	£120	Ann Duany
1820 April 6	William	10/	William Jam.s Witter
1821 Sept.r 17	Cath.e Raby	£100	John Raby
1822 March 5	George Munro	None	Eliz.th Munro
1822 January 20	Sarah Brown	10/	Phœbe James
1820 June 20	Bessy	None	Ann Reid Oliphant
1822 March 26	Alexander Hine	10/	Thomas Hine
April 2	Mary Copsey	£160	Ann Sill p.r atty
1813 Oct.r 30	Tom al Tom Langley	10/	Ann Fleming
1819 March 16	Frank al James Francis	10/	James Burnett
1820 Feb.y 23	Sarah Douglas	10/	Robert Urquhart
1818 Oct.r 16	John Correa	£120	Sarah De Campos
1821 April 23	Mary al Mary Jane Coldwell	£16	Elizabeth Allen

Above: An overseer watches work going on at a sugar mill in the West Indies, 1849.

Right: Pierre Dominique Toussaint l'Ouverture (1746–1803), black revolutionary leader and liberator of Haiti. Previously a slave, he died in prison in France after being tricked on board a French ship.

British finally evacuated the remnants of their invasion force in 1798, having lost 15,000 out of 25,000 men to a combination of rampant diseases and combat deaths.

By the end of that year only the forces of the mulatto leader, Rigaud, who controlled the southern peninsula, stood between Toussaint and total control of the country. The fighting between them was fierce, but under the black general, Dessalines, Toussaint's forces were victorious. After a decade of almost constant conflict the rebels had succeeded in taking control of the richest and most productive colony in the Caribbean. A French re-invasion force of some 44,000 troops sent by Napoleon to restore slavery was defeated in 1803, although it did succeed in kidnapping Toussaint, who died in a French dungeon in April.

Fears that this revolt would set a precedent for slave rebellions elsewhere were a constant worry for the planters and led to the extraordinary barbarity of the repressive measures imposed on slaves captured in the numerous other revolts that broke out intermittently in the Caribbean islands. Elsewhere, the terrain permitted substantial numbers of runaway slaves, known as maroons, to set up and maintain often quite large communities beyond the reach of the colonial authorities. After numerous unsuccessful attempts to subdue them the planter governments were forced to sign peace treaties with the maroon communities in the rugged interior of Jamaica and the rain forests of Guyana. In Spanish America there were numerous small maroon settlements known as *palenques* in remote or inaccessible areas, while in Brazil the rain forest sheltered many fugitive slaves in camps called *quilombos*. The largest of these, Palmares, established around 1605–1606, was virtually a separate mini state with a substantial capital. Ruled by a king, Zambi, it survived numerous Portuguese expeditions before it was finally overrun in November 1695.

Right: Two Creole girls from Surinam (Suriname) wearing traditional head kerchiefs, *anjisas*, which are starched and folded in various styles, often to indicate mood. Distinct African-American societies developed on the coast and in the interior of Surinam. The latter, populated by Maroons, descendants of runaway slaves, established a new hybrid version of African village society in the Americas.

Below: The San Domingo rebellion led by Toussaint l'Ouverture. The example set by the rebellion inspired blacks throughout the Americas, while terrifying slave holders and increasing the severity with which other revolts were suppressed.

Far right: A man begins to dance as part of a voodoo ceremony in a Haitian village. The Catholic church severed contact with Haiti for many decades following the revolution, allowing African-inspired religious traditions to thrive.

4 King Cotton: Planters, Paternalism, and Slavery in the American South

Slavery was crucial to the development of many of the colonies established in North America. It was the forced labor of Africans and African-Americans, assisted in some cases by that of impoverished Europeans imported as indentured servants, that opened up the vast new territories to the production of crops and laid the basis for the future prosperity of the United States. Today, the descendants of those original African survivors of the Middle Passage form a substantial percentage of the population, still struggling in many cases with the bitter legacy of racism and injustice left by the era of slavery. Yet the American colonies were relatively late in their involvement in the slave trade and accounted for a surprisingly low proportion of the total. It is only in the last few decades that scholars working with the details of historical records have established that the number of slaves imported into the mainland of North America was probably a little over half a million. This amounts to about six percent of the Atlantic slave trade, and is substantially lower than the figure for some of the larger Caribbean sugar plantation colonies such as Cuba. For only a brief period after the Revolution and before the abolition did the American colonies account for a substantial proportion of those Africans crossing the Atlantic.

Many American colonists, seeking to found new communities on ideals of liberty and equality that contrasted with the poverty and oppression they had left in Europe, were conscious of the disparity between these aspirations and the reality of a reliance on slave labor. Whilst this prevented neither the development of slave-based plantation economies in the American South, nor the direct and indirect involvement in slave trading by merchants in northern colonies, it did serve to stimulate both a continued undercurrent of legislative opposition in the post-Independence era and the elaboration of a self-justifying ideology of paternalism in the ante-bellum (i.e. pre-Civil War) South. Despite the many brutalities and the all-pervasive injustices, the worst excesses of plantation slavery in the Caribbean—with its appalling death toll of African lives—were far more rarely found. Taken as a whole, the slave societies of the North American mainland were the only ones in which a locally-born Creole

TO BE SOLD, on board the Ship *Bance-Island*, on tuesday the 6th of *May* next, at *Ashley-Ferry*; a choice cargo of about 250 fine healthy NEGROES, just arrived from the Windward & Rice Coast. —The utmost care has already been taken, and shall be continued, to keep them free from the least danger of being infected with the SMALL-POX, no boat having been on board, and all other communication with people from *Charles-Town* prevented. *Austin, Laurens, & Appleby.*

N. B. Full one Half of the above Negroes have had the SMALL-POX in their own Country.

Left: An advertisement for a slave auction.

To be SOLD by AUCTION,
On SATURDAY the 17th day of JANUARY inst.
At HAYNE HALL, near JACKSONBURGH,
Ninety valuable Negroes
Belonging to the Estate of the late
COLONEL ISAAC HAYNE.
Among the Men, are
DRIVERS, WHEELWRIGHTS,
CARPENTERS, COOPERS, &c.
Among the Women, are
HOUSE WENCHES, COOKS,
SEMPSTRESSES, WASHERWOMEN, &c.

Left: An auction poster announcing the sale of "90 Valuable Negroes," draws attention to the range of skilled tasks performed by slaves throughout the South.

population was able to sustain itself, despite the struggle to work and the constantly threatened heartbreak of forcibly separated families. That the black population rose from less than 7,000 in 1680 to 1,377,080 in the first post-abolition census of 1810 owes as much to natural increase as to slave importation.

Before the Revolution: Slavery in the American Colonies

There were small numbers of slaves in the mainland colonies, working as both domestic servants and agricultural laborers, almost from the first years of European settlement. Some of the earliest seem to have been bought by the Dutch. Records of a colonist, John Rolfe, cited by the historian James Rawley, noted the import of slaves in Virginia in 1619. This was, however, an isolated incident and it was with the spread of tobacco growing after about 1670 that more regular slave imports began. Before this the colonies had been largely reliant on white indentured servants. Mostly young men hoping to escape poverty in England, Germany, and Ireland, these servants were bound to work for their master for a fixed term, usually three to five years. A few were taught a trade but the majority were agricultural laborers. Masters worked them ruthlessly to extract the maximum possible labor before the contracted term expired. Contracts could be extended further as punishment for indebtedness or attempts to run away. Many did try to escape and suffered whippings, branding, or bodily mutilation if captured. About half of all indentured servants in the Chesapeake colonies died before their contracts expired. Once free, the shortage of women allowed most female servants to marry but men usually remained impoverished dependants of their former master.

After 1680, the settlers switched towards an increasing reliance on slave labor and the number of new indentured servants fell in both proportional and absolute terms. The percentage of Africans in the population of Virginia rose from seven to forty-four percent, and that of South Carolina from seventeen to sixty-one percent in the years between 1680 and 1750. In part this was due to changing circumstances in the domestic labor market in England, that reduced the supply and raised the cost of indentured workers. At much the same time British merchants, in the form of the chartered Royal Africa Company, opened up access to the Atlantic slave trade on a wider scale. In simple economic terms, the relative price of slaves improved markedly, although it remained more expensive to buy a slave than to take on an indentured servant. Slaves, however, could be kept in perpetual servitude and so represented a better long term investment. Moreover, it was generally felt that they were better suited to labor conditions and so more likely to survive. It was also felt to be more difficult for slaves to escape successfully as it was harder for them to blend in with the free poor—the presumption, despite the presence of growing numbers of free blacks, was that all Africans were slaves.

There was, at first, a degree of uncertainty about the legal position of these newly imported slaves. Many slaveholders were particularly reluctant to allow their slaves to become Christians in case it should subsequently be established that this was a cause for emancipation. However, beginning with Virginia's first major slave code in 1680, laws were enacted over the following decades by both southern and northern colonies that restricted the rights of both slaves and free blacks. Slaves and the children of slave women were bound for life; they required written permission to carry arms or leave their master's land; and

Right: The premises of Price Birch & Co., slave dealers, photographed during the Civil War.

the possibilities of manumission were severely constrained. Free blacks were prevented from voting, from marrying whites, and from testifying in court against whites. Scholars have argued that these evolving laws reflect both increasing racial prejudice and the growing dominance of the interests of slave-holders on whose continued prosperity the colonies were dependent. There is considerable evidence that in the early years and in frontier zones of spreading colonization, blacks and poor whites interacted on a much more tolerant basis than would later become the norm. Isolated cases of slaves marrying poor white women have been documented from seventeenth century Virginia.

The circumstances of their labor were the dominant factors in determining the differing life experiences and the possibilities of community development facing slaves in differing regions. Only a minority worked in conditions similar to those of sugar plantation slaves in the Caribbean. It was only in South Carolina and Georgia, where the large scale irrigation needed for rice growing (similar to the demands of sugar cultivation) required a large and intensively worked labor force, that holdings of 100 or more slaves became commonplace by the late eighteenth century.

Absentee planters on these estates, and those that subsequently developed to produce cotton on the Sea Islands, usually used the "task" system, under which each slave was set a job for the day and was free to stop once he or she had completed it. As in the Caribbean, this permitted the slaves to develop a substantial area of economic independence, and for this reason alone it was not popular

with planters elsewhere in the South. Tobacco, the dominant crop of Virginia and Maryland, did not require the same concentration of labor. More than half the slaveholders in this area owned five or fewer slaves, living and working in far closer contact with the master than was normal on the minority of large plantations. Significant proportions of the white population in most districts owned no slaves at all. The plantation aristocracy of large scale slave owners, important and influential though they were in Southern society, were by no means the norm. In the North there were a very few large estates and the overwhelming majority of slaves worked as servants, craftsmen, or farm hands, owned in groups of only two or three. Slaves performed a wide variety of skilled tasks. In Virginia in 1648 one master was reported to have available for hire as skilled workers over forty slaves pursuing various trades. Although this was far from typical, as the number of white laborers increased so did hostility to the competition posed by the hiring out of slaves in this way. Nevertheless, the contribution made to local economies by the labor skills of both slaves working on the plantations and those living in towns was considerable.

Revolution and Independence: A False Dawn for Abolition

The era of the American Revolution has been described as bringing the first major challenge to American slavery. Thousands of slaves were able to take advantage of opportunities the disruptions of war offered to make a break for freedom. Of perhaps greater long term importance, the whole institution of slavery, which had previously seemed beyond reproach, became the focus of sustained criticism. In turn this provoked slavery's apologists to advance new claims in its defense, and although this is hard to quantify, perhaps stimulated a gradual alleviation of some of the worst hardships of slave conditions. These defensive moves succeeded in re-entrenching slavery in the South, and assisted in its expansion as new states were colonized to the west. The decades immediately following the Revolutionary War, as we saw in the previous chapter, saw the largest sustained importation of new slaves in American history.

In his recent history of American slavery, Peter Kolchin has outlined a number of developments that combined to cast doubt on the previously almost unchallenged acceptance of slavery as a social institution. He points in particular to the rapidly changing climate of intellectual life in Europe and America from the mid-eighteenth century. Usually called the Enlightenment and closely associated with advances in both scientific and economic rationalism, intellectuals in this period began to question received ideas on such important issues as cruelty, and the appropriate treatment of fellow human beings.

The notion of human rights began to be expressed for the first time during this period. Attitudes to the unrestricted infliction of punishments on the human body began to change. Many of these then novel ideas found expression in the Declaration of Independence and the newly drafted constitution for the independent United States.

While many seemed to have no problem with exempting blacks in general and slaves in particular from these newly valued rights, others called into question the whole fabric of ideas about the supposedly natural inferiority of Africans that had grown up in the justification of the slave trade. Perhaps, they suggested, the so-called "slavishness" they perceived in the contacts with blacks was a consequence of slavery and not some natural moral condition. Isolated cases of clearly intellectually talented slaves, such as the poet Phillis Wheatley, and the mathematician Benjamin Bannecker, excited great interest. Thomas Jefferson wrote of the latter in 1791:

"I shall be delighted to see these instances of moral eminence so multiplied as to prove that the want of talents observed in them is merely the effect of their degraded condition, and not proceeding from any difference in the structure of the parts on which intellect depends."

Eighteenth century thinkers came to regard the newly elaborated economic principles of free trade, the primacy of the market, and freedom of contract, outlined in Adam Smith's influential book *The Wealth of Nations* (1776), as

Below: The slave market on the harbor at New York. It was at these harborside markets in often hectic scenes that terrified newly landed Africans were sold to their first masters.

not just natural laws but moral imperatives. The contradictions between slavery and these new tenets were arguable, but seemed increasingly apparent, providing a ready explanation both for specific crises such as struck the tobacco growing areas, and more general malaise such as the perceived inefficiency of slave labor. Religious sentiments, as we see when we consider the abolition movement in the following chapter, also played a key part in calling into question the "peculiar institution" in the South. Both the Quakers' intellectual opposition to slavery and the growing unease displayed by some members of the Methodist and Baptist churches as religious revivals spread through the South in the closing decades of the century were increasingly important factors. The founding fathers of the independence movement moved in the climate of these new ideas, and were, to differing degrees, profoundly influenced by them. Although slavery was to continue to

Left: Thomas Jefferson (1743–1826), a leading figure in the application of Enlightenment philosophy to American political life and principal drafter of the Declaration of Independence, was nevertheless a believer in the racial inferiority of Africans. Although in retirement he corresponded with leading Abolitionists, he declined to free his own slaves.

Below: "The First Cotton Gin."

Cuba: Corte de Caña.
Cutting Sugar Cane.

Above: Nineteenth century photograph of cane cutters at work on a Cuban sugar plantation.

Below: The waterfront at Charleston, South Carolina.

Charleston, S.C., East Battery, showing Waterfront.

years were promised their freedom. Other slaves were obliged to enlist in place of their masters. More significant, though, was the effect of an appeal made in November 1775 by the Governor of Virginia, promising freedom to slaves who took up arms with the British. Although only a few thousand were ever able to reach British forces and take up this offer, and many of these perished from small-pox and other diseases, throughout much of the South slaves took advantage of the turmoil to flee in huge numbers. It has been estimated that in South Carolina, for example, slave-holders lost some thirty percent of all their slaves, and no doubt a considerably higher proportion of adult males.

Left: Black slave drivers occupied an anomalous and complex position in the cotton plantations of the South, often hated by their fellow slaves.

Below: An early image of the fortified settlement of Charleston, South Carolina, dating from 1673. At this time indentured Europeans still provided the main source of labor in the North American colonies.

flourish for several more generations, it could never again be taken for granted.

If the intellectual climate of the age challenged the slave system, the circumstances of the war itself offered many slaves a more immediate and concrete prospect of liberty. Although calls were made by rebels to arm the slaves and allow them to fight in exchange for their freedom, opposition from planter interests succeeded in suppressing any effective proposals that would lead to organized participation by slaves on any scale. Slave enlistment was permitted in Maryland, and in New York slaves who served for three

One of the most marked effects of the Revolutionary era was to translate the economic divide that had long existed between the slave-based societies of the South and the states of the North, where slavery was economically marginal, into a growing sense of a moral and social divide based on attitudes towards slavery. While action taken in the states of the upper South, such as Virginia, Delaware,

Above: A scene from the 1927 film version of *Uncle Tom's Cabin*.

and Maryland, to ease some of their slave laws, such as the restriction on manumission, had some effect (in Delaware for example three quarters of blacks were free by 1810,) the legal basis of slavery was upheld. In contrast, Northern states, where slavery was far less economically important, began to pass graduated emancipation acts, allowing all slaves born after the passage of the acts to become free once they reached adulthood. As half-hearted as these measures were, in combination with an increasing tendency towards voluntary manumission by Northern slave-holders, they ensured that virtually all Northern blacks were free by the early decades of the nineteenth century. These acts were augmented at the national level by passage of laws barring the extension of slavery in newly colonized areas, such as the act of 1787 covering the present states of Ohio, Michigan, Indiana, Illinois, and Wisconsin. Both Congress and a number of states moved to prohibit the import of new slaves, although Congress was prevented by a compromise agreement at the Constitutional Convention of 1787 from introducing such a ban until 1807. It was this delay that allowed the planter-dominated states of the lower South to make the following two decades a new peak for American involvement in transatlantic slave trading.

Cotton, Paternalism, and Plantation Slavery

For the majority of blacks in the South the hopes for freedom aroused during the Revolution were to prove illusory. Despite the growing hostility in the North, slavery lived on, apparently strengthened and extending across a massive new region of the continent. The key to this expansion, and to the surge in demand for slaves, was cotton. The development of the cotton gin in 1793 prompted a rapid expansion of cotton growing across the Southern states and financed the opening up of huge new areas to agriculture. From a mere 3,000 bales in 1790, cotton production rose to 178,000 by 1810, and exploded to over four million bales by 1860. By this time it was overwhelmingly the largest export of the United States, and it both fed the textile mills of England and laid the basis for the subsequent industrialization of America. Over the same period there was a comparable dramatic surge in the number of slaves, from 697,897 in 1790 to some four million by 1860. Around a million of these slaves were forcibly relocated to supply the labor needed to open up the new cotton-growing states to the west. An internal slave trade developed, breaking up families and slave communities. Once again, large plantations with 100 or more slaves were exceptional, the majority working quite close to their masters on properties with fifty or fewer slaves. Frederick Law Olmsted, who published an account of his travels through the South in the 1850s, noted details of both large and small plantations. As well as the elegant

83

Chartered by the Legislature of South Carolina.

No. 4185   B   B   No. 4185   20

THE COTTON PLANTERS LOAN ASSOCIATION

of the Fifth Congressional District of South Carolina

Will pay to W Dawkins or Bearer

TWENTY DOLLARS

Unionville S. C. 13 May 186_

Treas.   Pres.

Secured by a Pledge of Cotton at Six Cents per Pound for the Amount of the Issue, as well as the private Property of the Stockholders.

Redeemable in Gold within Six Months after the raising of the Blockade on our Coast.

P. W. BORNEMANN, CHARLESTON S.C.

No. 210   No. 210   5   5

G EO

FARMERS & EXCHANGE BANK

OF CHARLESTON

Will pay FIVE DOLLARS to Bearer

on demand. Charleston, S.C. 13 Sept 1853

Cash.   Pres.

Toppan Carpenter Casilear & Co. Phila & New York.

white-pillared great houses on large estates of 1,500 or more acres, he saw far more modest establishments. One such was:

"a small square log cabin, with a broad open shed or piazza in front, and a chimney made of sticks and mud, leaning against one end. A smaller detached cabin, 20 feet in the rear was used for a kitchen . . . About the house was a large yard, in which were two or three China trees, and two fine Cherokee roses; half a dozen hounds; several black babies; turkeys, and chickens; and a pet sow . . . Three hundred yards from the house was a gin house and stable, and in the interval between were two rows of comfortable Negro cabins."

However, it was the big planters in their great houses with their retinues of domestic servants and field hands, who framed the ruling ideology of slavery in the South. Lesser slave-holders and poor whites took a lead from them. Particularly after the emergence of an overwhelmingly American-born slave population, less alien to the planters in the culture and more or less adapted to the circumstances of slave life, planters came to view the slaves in a different way. Taking a lead from those who were resident with their family on their plantations for much of the year, interacting on a daily basis with both domestic slaves and field hands, it became normal for the slave-holders to extend the idea of family to their slaves and think of themselves as benevolent patriarchs, presiding, sternly but justly, over often recalcitrant "children."

In response to the growing attacks of Northern abolitionists, they asserted that their slaves were not only happy and contented, but far better off than if they had been free. They pointed not just to the alleged advantages of their position compared with their fate as slaves or war victims in Africa (ignoring the extent of the contribution the slave trade had made to the promotion of these in Africa itself,) but to the relatively far worse material conditions of the laboring poor in areas of Europe transformed by the Industrial Revolution. While the self-serving nature of these arguments, and the facility with which they glossed over the continued brutalities of slave life were readily apparent, the nature of the relationships that developed between slave-holders and slaves was a complex one, often filled with mixed emotions on both sides. There is ample evidence that real affection did develop, that many masters and mistresses, however self-deluded about the cares and woes of looking after "their people" did in many cases take real trouble and undergo considerable expense, for example in securing medical treatment for favored slaves. As abolitionists pointed out, of course, favored treatment of a few failed to mitigate even the continued injustice of their position, let alone the hardship and exploitation suffered by the many. But that was not how the planters saw it. They generally took a keen and detailed interest in all aspects of their slaves' lives.

Below: Black workers plant sweet potatoes on James Hopkinson's plantation, Edisto Island, North Carolina.

Left: A slave family, South Carolina.

Below: A colonnaded plantation house in the old South. In fact only a minority of slaves worked on big plantations, many more were settled in smaller groups on less wealthy farms.

many instances he cites a letter from a Mrs Mary Jones, a plantation owner's wife, written in 1866 "My life long (I mean since I had a home) I have been laboring and caring for them, and since the war have labored with all my might to supply their wants, and expended everything I had on their support, directly and indirectly; and this is their return." It was particularly painful to many that it was often their most trusted and favored confidants that incited the other slaves to desert to the Union lines.

As for the slaves, their attitudes to the masters were often ambiguous. The same masters who beat them and split up their families could protect them from the ravages of the slave patrols manned by brutal poor whites. In keeping with the paternalist ethos, many masters made a point of personally handing out the rations of food and distributions of clothing, while hiding behind their overseer to administer punishments. Many slaves and former slaves demonstrated considerable, and we might consider unjustified, loyalty to their master and his family in the Civil War and its aftermath. Perhaps the best anecdotal

Numerous diaries and correspondence make clear their very real feelings of shock and hurt when favored slaves ran away or committed some other offence. The extent to which they had deceived themselves was only revealed in the Civil War, which Eugene Genovese in his classic book *Roll, Jordan Roll,* called "the moment of truth." Among

A MAP OF THE DANISH ISLAND St CROIX, in the West Indies Surveyed 1799 by P.L. Oxholm. Drawn from the Original Map.

West Indies Nº 2

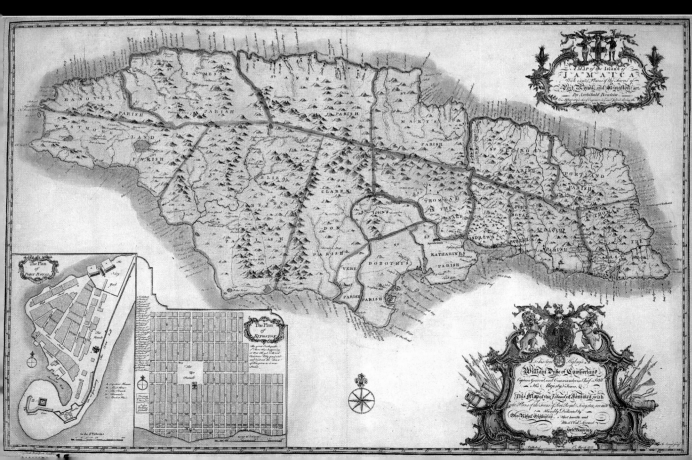

A MAP of the Island of JAMAICA

The Plan of PORT ROYAL

The Plan of KINGSTON

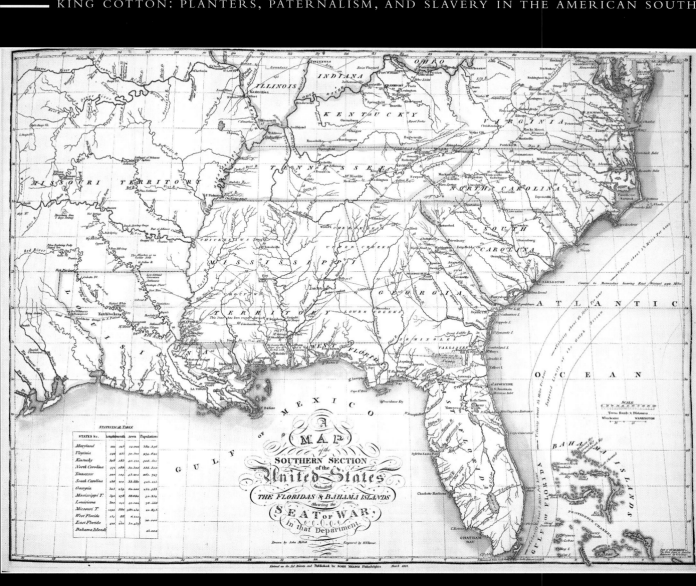

Above left: The Danish island of St. Croix in 1809, the tabular material on the survey gives a detailed breakdown of the .population. There were at this time 2,223 whites, 1,164 colored, and 25,452 negroes. They produced 18,714 pounds of sugar, 838,100 gallons of rum, and 16,000 pounds of cotton per annum.

Left: Jamaica in 1753, a map dedicated to William, Duke of Cumberland, better known for his role as commander-in-chief of the Stuart army that defeated Bonnie Prince Charlie's forces at Culloden. Along with Barbados, Jamaica was Britain's main sugar producer. In Jamaica it was estimated that, between 1655 and 1737, of the 676,276 slaves recorded on arrival, 31,181 died while still in the harbor.

account of these ambiguities and the fears they provoked in the slave-holders is provided by an incident cited by Genovese. An anxious mistress asked one of her favored slaves if they would cut her throat when the Union troops arrived. She can hardly have been reassured by his answer that they would not. Instead, they would go to the neighboring plantation and kill the master there, while the neighbor's slaves would call to deal with her!

Moving behind the self-serving ideology of the slave-holders, life for plantation slaves in the American South was hard. People struggled to build and sustain a family, a community, and a religious and cultural life, while fulfilling the work demanded of them in a way that would avoid the ever-threatened punishments. Field labor was the lot of the majority of slaves on the plantations. The amount of work this required varied according to the seasons and the pace of the crop. Generally planters favored the "gang" system in which a group of slaves, both male and female, supervised by a driver appointed from their own ranks, worked from sunrise to sunset. In the hottest times a two-hour break might be allowed following the midday meal. As slave owners constantly complained, it was rarely possible to compel these gangs to work as fast or as efficiently as desired. A white overseer organized the gangs and set the pattern of labor, but would rarely bother to supervise directly except in crucial periods such as the harvest season. At such times the normal hours of work would be extended and pressure exerted through both

additional punishments and the prospects of a festival meal on completion. Normally field workers had Sundays off, and in some cases Saturday afternoons, and planters who tried to deny their slaves these accepted rights risked stirring up considerable counterproductive resentment. When Sunday work was needed at exceptionally busy periods, some masters paid the slaves small sums. Few plantations were large enough to provide full-time work for slaves with such specialized skills as carpentry and metalwork but most had one or more slaves who could carry out these tasks when required. In some cases they were hired out to neighboring planters, and in their free time could earn money for themselves. Some plantations, however, sustained a whole array of such specialist slaves, making them virtually independent of the surrounding community for their labor needs. George Washington's home house in 1786, for example, had four carpenters, four spinners, three drivers and stablemen, two smiths, two seamstresses, a waggoner, a carter, and a gardener.

Scholars have now recognized that the old image of house servants on the plantations as a privileged and favored elite was oversimplified. It is true that many of them benefited from their closeness to the master's family to secure benefits, from material items such as better clothing to less tangible but much prized access to opportunities for education. However, although some did, undoubtedly, arouse considerable resentment by showing a sense of superiority to their fellow slaves, for the majority

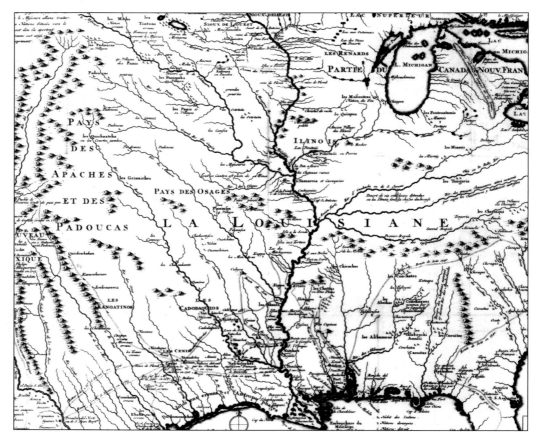

Right: Map showing the Europeans' expedition and settlements in Louisiana. The opening up of new states following the purchase of these territories from France was a major cause of dispute between the representatives of slave-holding and free states in Congress in the years before the Civil War.

Left: Slaves operating a cotton-gin.

evidence suggests that the other workers themselves did not have a particularly high view of the household slaves, reserving their respect for those such as black preachers, midwives, folk doctors and the literate. The "Mammy," the archetypal black matriarchal figure who effectively ran many plantation households, overseeing the domestic arrangements and the raising of the master's children, was a special case to the slave-holders, but perhaps often as much feared as respected by the slaves. As for the drivers, selected from among the slaves to supervise and control their fellows, they have generally been reviled by historians although as Genovese notes they "ran the gamut from sadistic monsters to compassionate leaders of their people."

Life on the plantations certainly provided plenty of opportunity for the sadistic, whether they were masters, overseers, or slave drivers. Planters saw the regular use of both the threat and the reality of physical punishments as essential to enforce their labor requirements, regarding their slaves as naturally lazy and ill-disciplined. Beyond this, however, most slave owners, as part of their paternalistic ethos, regarded it as their role to supervise and regulate all aspects of the lives of their "people" and often laid down a vast panoply of rules governing the most petty

the role had its own risks and disadvantages. Unlike the field hands they were constantly at the beck and call of the master and his family, in many cases having to sleep in the big house, sometimes even in the same room as the master or mistress. Such close contacts provided endless occasions to offend the master or transgress the numerous petty rules bringing punishments for offences that in field hands would have largely escaped notice. For the women and girls the exposure to sexual exploitation was an ever present danger with the master and his sons ready to take predatory advantage of their enforced proximity. As Harriet Jacob's account in her classic autobiography *Incidents in the Life of a Slave Girl* illustrates, in these circumstances constant intimidation and pressure to submit was more frequent than outright rape. Moreover, in a society where sexual liaisons with slaves, however widespread, were publicly frowned upon, and the jealousy of the mistress a real danger, the victims and their children were as likely to be sold away as freed. These women, and slave women as a whole, have recently been characterized as suffering under a triple burden of slavery, race, and gender. Household slaves generally had close family links and personal ties among the field hands, and except on the largest and wealthiest of plantations could expect to be sent to assist them in the fields at harvest times. The

SOUTHERN COTTON PLANTATION.
"Knowing thy master also is in heaven."

Right: Prints illustrating workers on a cotton plantation and the houses of a plantation slave quarters.

1604 Birds Eye View, Charleston, S. C.

a city full of historical relic + wealth
nov. 19/09

Above left: The slave quarters on a southern plantation.

Left: A view of Charleston in 1604.

Above: The plantation house. Relations between the house slaves and those who worked the fields were often strained.

Right: A street in New Orleans.

offences. The few exceptional masters who refused to chastise their slaves, and those who went to the other extreme and beat people to death without an acceptable "excuse," could expect to be subject to social pressure from their neighbors and peers to conform to more normal conduct, as both were thought to risk unsettling the slave population of the entire district. Slaves were whipped and flogged regularly, with few escaping at least one serious whipping in a lifetime, and a substantial proportion suffering many more. Women were generally as severely whipped as men, and both sexes could be stripped half naked for a public beating at a moment's notice. The scars left frequently lasted a lifetime. Olmsted watched the flogging of an eighteen year old girl accused by the overseer of trying to miss a day's work. She received "thirty or forty blows across the shoulder" with a raw-hide whip, and was then beaten again for refusing to admit her fault. Most slaves, demonstrating the human capacity to adapt to even the most brutal conditions, generally accepted the majority of punishments provided they could see that they were imposed for an accepted reason. What aroused great anger and resentment, and often caused the slave directly involved to risk all by running away, was any excessive breach in the accepted customs governing punishments, or a clearly unjust or arbitrary display of cruelty. Slaves who ran away, or committed other serious offences such as killing a fellow slave or overseer, were subjected to the

almost unrestricted exercise of violence by the master. While, in law at least, he could not kill them outright without risking some legal reprisal, any beating or mutilation could be imposed, whether or not it subsequently lead to death. The threat of being sold away and losing all contact with family and friends was also a potent one, hanging over all and used to discipline the most uncooperative of slaves.

In addition to the impromptu punishments administered on the plantations, the legal codes of slave states laid down a long list of offences for which slaves would be hanged, with an equally lengthy further list prescribing precisely how many lashes they were to receive for lesser offences. Despite occasional legal recognition of the logical incompatibility of confining slaves to the legal status of chattels and at the same time holding them responsible for their actions, the overwhelming dominance of planter interests meant that the few attempts at legal reform made slow progress. Although the laws also laid certain obligations on the masters regarding the treatment of slaves, these could only rarely be enforced. One of the

Below: Richard Allen founded the African Methodist Episcopal Denomination. The reluctance of many white churches to accommodate the needs of black Christians, and their often ambivalent attitudes towards slavery, led to the foundation of independent black churches.

Maryland Legalizes Slavery

In the second half of the seventeenth century the English colonies in North America passed acts to define the legal status of slaves and restrict their involvement with whites:

"Bee itt Enacted by the Right Honble the Lord Proprietary by the aduice and Consent of the upper and lower housed of this present Generall Assembly That all Negroes or other slaves already within the Prouince And all Negroes and other slaves to bee hereafter imported into the Province shall serve Durante Vita [service for life]. And all Children born of any Negroe or other slave shall be Slaves as their fathers were for the terme of their lives. And forasmuch as divers freeborne English women forgetfull of their Condicion and to the disgrace of our Nation doe inter marry with Negro Slaves by which alsoe divers suited may arise touching the Issue of such woemen and a great damage doth befall the Masters of such Negroes for prevention whereof for deterring such freeborne women from such shamefull Matches Bee itt further Enacted by the Authority advice and consent aforesaid. That whatsoever free borne woman shal inter marry with any slave from and after the last day of this present Assembly shall Serve the master of such slave dureing the life of her husband And that all the issue of such freeborne woemen soe marryed shall be Slaves as their fathers were. And Bee itt further Enacted that all the Issues of English or other freeborne woemen that have already marryed Negroes shall serve the Masters of their Parents till they be Thirty yeares of age and noe longer."

Left: Slaves making indigo.

95

Right: A nineteenth century
photograph of the slave
woman "Aunt Edie."

Above: Cotton pickers and their overseer.

Left: Slaves in a cotton field.

most significant legal disabilities, hindering almost any effort by slaves to obtain a fair hearing, was that they were prohibited from giving evidence against whites. Nevertheless, as Genovese has pointed out, by comparison with the grotesque absurdities of racist bias in the enforcement of Southern legal systems in the long period of lynchings and the Ku Klux Klan that followed abolition, slaves on trial for alleged offences of the murder or rape of whites did sometimes receive a surprisingly open hearing.

In the face of the pervasive threat of brutal punishment that hung over plantation slaves, it can hardly be surprising that many attempted to resist or to run away. There were a few attempts at real slave rebellions, the best known of which were the Stono rebellion near Charleston in 1739, and those led by Gabriel Prosser in Virginia in 1800, Denmark Vesey in South Carolina in 1822, and Nat Turner also in Virginia in 1831. Fifty-nine whites were killed by Turner's men, but they were all rapidly defeated and savage reprisals by terrified whites followed. The revolts were,

Slaves in Transit

In the early decades of the nineteenth century the vast expansion of slavery into new states promoted by the boom in cotton production lead to an internal slave trade which split up families and sent coffles of chained prisoners on long and arduous journeys. George W. Featherstonehaugh, an English geographer employed by the U.S. War Department as a land surveyor, observed one of these coffles in 1834:

"Just as we reached new River, in the early gray of the morning, we came up with a singular spectacle, the most striking one of the kind I have ever witnessed. It was a camp of negro slave-drivers, just packing up to start; they had about three hundred slaves with them, who had bivouacked the preceding night in chains in the woods; these they were conducting to Natchez, upon the Mississippi River, to work upon the sugar plantations in Lousiana. It resembled one of those coffles of slaves spoken of by Mungo Park, except that they had a caravan of nine waggons and single-horse carriages, for the purpose of conducting the white people, and any of the blacks that should fall lame, to which they were now putting the horses to pursue their march. The female slaves were, some of them, sitting on logs of wood, whilst others were standing and a great many little black

Right: A slave coffle passing the Capitol. The huge growth in cotton production throughout the South in the first half of the nineteenth century generated a new internal slave trade in which massive numbers of African-American slaves suffered arduous forced marches to open up the cotton growing regions on the expanding frontiers of settlement.

Far right, top: A slave owner overseeing cotton pickers at work in Texas, 1800.

Far right, bottom: Slave chain: walking through the bush, children and adults in a slave chain gang, shackled by their necks and hands. An overseer with a gun walks beside them.

children were warming themselves at the fires of the bivouac. In front of them all, and prepared for the march, stood, in double files, about 200 male slaves, manacled and chained to each other. I had never seen so revolting a sight before! . . . To make this spectacle still more disgusting and hideous, some of the principal white slave drivers, who were tolerably well dressed . . . were standing near, laughing and smoking.

"Wishing them in my heart all manner of evil to endure . . . we drove on, and having forded the river in a flat-bottomed boat, drew up on the road, where I persuaded the driver to wait until we had witnessed the crossing of the river by the "gang," as it was called.

"It was an interesting, but a melancholy spectacle, to see them effect the passage of the river: first, a man on horseback selected a shallow place in the ford for the male slaves: then followed a waggon and four horses, attended by another man on horseback. The other waggons contained the children and some that were lame, whilst the scows, or flatboats, crossed the women and some of the people belonging to the caravan. There was much method and vigilance observed, for this was one of the situations where the gangs—always watchful to obtain their liberty—often show a disposition to mutiny, knowing that if one or

two of them could wrench their manacles off; they could soon free the rest, and either disperse themselves or overpower and slay their sordid keepers, and fly to the Free States. The slave-drivers, aware of this disposition in the unfortunate negroes, endeavor to mitigate their discontent by feeding them well on the march, and by encouraging them to sing "Old Virginia never tire," to the banjo."

however, just the most visible feature of a mostly more limited but effective pattern of resistance and non-cooperation. Individual slaves often fought back against brutal overseers, arbitrary punishments, or assaults on women. Overseers, and more rarely masters, were killed on numerous occasions, and the knowledge of this must have acted as a constraint on the excesses of others. Runaways, who risked death at the hands of the slave patrols of poor whites and their ferocious dogs, and often vicious punishment if returned to their master, either set out for the "free" states or Canada, or remained close to the plantation aided clandestinely by friends and family. Many of the latter ran away as a protest at some specific grievance and masters often negotiated their return. Still more common was a form of limited everyday resistance, manifested in slow working, feigned stupidity, and general non-cooperation.

The successful building of a family and community life in slavery was the key to the remarkable expansion in the slave population of the South in the ante-bellum years. They were, as we have seen, despite the hardship of plantation life, the only slave community in the Americas able to reproduce itself in this way. The slave quarters, usually a cluster of small two-room houses set some distance away from the planter's house, provided the main site where these families could develop. Usually made from logs daubed with mud, with shuttered windows, these rudimentary and uncomfortable houses mostly accommodated a family unit of four to six adults and children. Most took considerable pride in maintaining these houses, using their spare time to make furniture, add on stock pens, and improvise a range of household items to add to those bought with their scanty savings or acquired from the planter's cast-offs. Olmsted provided the following evocative picture of life in the slave quarters of a Mississippi plantation: "During the evening all the cabins were illuminated by great fires, and looking into one of them, I saw a very picturesque family group; a man sat on the ground making a basket, a woman lounged on a chest in the chimney corner smoking a pipe, and a boy and two girls sat in a bed which had been drawn up opposite her, completing the fireside circle. They were talking and laughing cheerfully." Near the quarters the slaves had small gardens where they could work in the evenings and on Sundays, in which they could raise corn and vegetables to supplement the rations distributed by the planter, and, in some cases, even raise modest amounts of cash crops for sale. Planters often commented bitterly in their correspondence on the amount of energy and initiative the men and women put into working their gardens compared with their lacklustre performance in the daytime. An alternative slave economy developed, although it never took on the scale found in Jamaica, in which slaves marketed their crops and those who had special skills in areas such as sewing, baking, or carpentry were sometimes able to accumulate considerable sums.

Although masters had an obvious financial interest in encouraging their slaves to have children, the majority allowed the young people to select their own marriage partners. They did however prefer that their slaves married within the plantation wherever possible, believing that off-plantation unions encouraged divided loyalty and provided too ready an excuse for slaves to be moving around the countryside. Nevertheless, enough masters attempted to intervene and impose marriages with partners of their choosing for it to be a regular event and a recurring source of bitterness. Of more general concern was the fact that slave marriages, even if blessed by a preacher, had no legal validity. They were often celebrated by both the planter's family and the slaves with considerable festivity and feasting, and any subsequent adultery was

Left: A shackled slave wearing an iron collar designed to prevent him from lying down.

Zamba Describes a Sale

Zamba, the prince sold into slavery, left this vivid description of the process of selling slaves in America:

"Several dray-loads of clothing for the slaves were brought alongside. Next day was still cold; but the whole of the slaves were put ashore, and obliged to wash and scour themselves. They were then provided with tolerably good clothing, made of blue or white coarse woollen cloth, of English manufacture, commonly called 'plains.' The owners of the ship had provided these; but, had the weather been warm, the poor slaves would have been put up for sale in the scanty clothing they were in. The captain told me they were advertised for sale, which would take place in two days. Meantime we had a considerable number of white gentlemen to visit us, mostly intending purchasers. On the appointed day, the auctioneer, a Mr Naylor, accompanied by two young clerks, came down; and, after much careful inspection, arranged the whole cargo in separate lots, some of them singly, and others in lots of fifteen or twenty. The single ones were intended for domestic servants in town, and were chosen from the youngest and smartest-looking; the larger lots for the country; or what are called 'field hands.' At length, a great number of white gentlemen had arrived, and a few white ladies—at least, white women; for their conduct was not such as would entitle them to be called ladies in Europe: in a calm, cool, business-like way, they went around the various groups of negroes, examining and handling their limbs in the same manner as I afterwards saw butchers examining cattle.

"The sale soon began, and took up a considerable time; the prices ranging from 250 to 450 dollars a head: the 32 negroes whom I had put on board brought nearly 10,000 dollars. it will be thus seen that the owners of the ship had made an excellent speculation: by this trip, as I learned from the captain, they had cleared from 90,000 to 100,000 dollars; and it must be allowed, that great part of this arose from the prudent and humane treatment which was exercised towards the live cargo. No doubt exists in my mind, that the moving principle in all concerned was avarice; and, in this case, it showed that, even from sinister motives, Providence can cause good to be produced at last. In the course of my subsequent experience, I have known ships, of the same tonnage as the Triton, arrive from Africa, in which 750 slaves had been embarked; but, owing to cruel usage, scanty and unwholesome provisions, impure air, and absolute filth, which prevailed on board, not more than 400 lived to reach Charleston; and of these, one-half were in a most weakly and miserable condition, and the remainder could by no means be classed as sound and healthy. In these cases, greed and avarice joined to inhumanity were punished; but at a sad expense of life, as regarded the wretched negroes. I have seen a slave-ship arrive from Africa, in such a condition as to its freight of flesh and blood, that no mortal of ordinary nerves could put his head below the hatch; and in such a miserable state were the negroes, that I have know 30 or 40 out of one cargo sent up to the hospital in carts. I heard frequently also, from what I deemed good authority, that on board these crowded and ill-conducted slavers, it was not a rare circumstance for the captain to order such poor slaves as were evidently dying, to be thrown overboard during the night, while yet the pulse of life was beating!"

The Lashing House

M. D. Conway, a white Virginian, recorded the regular administration of the lash in his home town:

"In the towns and villages the flogging is done by a special and legally-appointed functionary. It is only under severe emergencies or in the heat of passion that gentlemen and ladies beat their own slaves. The gentlemen shun it as a temporary descent to the social grade of the overseer or the constable, as the slave-whipper is called, and the ladies have too much sensibility to inflict complete chastisement; so they merely write on a bit of note-paper, 'Mr . . . , will you give Negro-girl Nancy . . . lashes, and charge to account . . .'

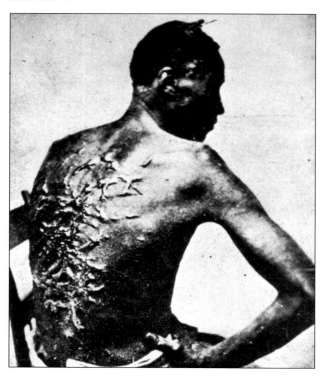

"I remember no building in our village so well as the slave-whipper's old, prison-like quarters, built of brick and limestone; and I recall vividly the fascination it had for myself and the other boys. It was known as 'Captain Pickett's.' The Captain himself, with his hard, stony look, and his iron gray hair and beard, was the very animal to inhabit such a shell . . .

"About this particular building we lingered and peered with an insatiable curiosity, all the more pertinaciously for being so often driven or dragged away. And our curiosity found enough fuel to keep it inflamed; for few hours ever passed without bringing some victim to his door . . . Around each victim we crowded, and when he or she disappeared and the door was shut, we—the boys—would rush around to all the walls, crevices, and backyards which we knew so well, gaining many a point from which we could see the half-naked cowering slave and the falling lash, and hear, with short-lived awe, the blows and the imploring tones, swelling to cries as the flogging proceeded.

"Perhaps at that moment some tourist from Old or New England travelling through the South to ascertain 'the facts' about Slavery, is at the hospital board of the writhing slave's owner, learning how merciful the treatment of the slave is. He will write in his Diary, that, during several weeks passed at the residence of this or that large slaveholder, he saw no cases of severe punishment, though he observed keenly. He does not know to this day, perhaps, that in every Southern community there is a 'Captain Pickett's place,'—a dark and unrevealed closet, connected by blind ways with the elegant mansions. His Diary might have had a different entry had he consulted the slaves or the boys . . .

"The slave-whipper is well paid for his ugly work, and makes a 'handsome living.' But the silent old man of whom I have been writing came at last to prefer no living at all to such a one; for one day a sobbing girl, bearing in her hand an order for forty lashes, was unable to gain admittance; whereupon the neighbours broke down the door, and found that Captain Picket had hung himself by his own whipping-post."

Left: Whip scars. Historians have suggested that virtually every slave faced being whipped at least once, while many were subjected to brutal whippings repeatedly.

Left: Slaves operating a baling machine.

Below: A slave auction in Montgomery, Alabama.

taken as a serious matter by all parties, but the union created could be dissolved at will by the master if it suited him to sell one of the partners. Pregnant women and nursing mothers were expected to work for all but a few weeks, with young children often bringing babies to the fields to be suckled. From birth until about the age of twelve or so children played around the house together with those of the master, supervised only by the older children. Often they had to scramble for food at lunch time from a communal trough in the yard. Perhaps the most important lesson they had to learn emerges repeatedly from slave narratives—their parents coached them again and again in the ways of appeasing the master and avoiding the scourge of his whip. Their childhood came to an abrupt end when the master decided they were old enough to be sent to the fields. At this point, too, if as happened all too often he was short of funds, they could be sold away. Masters did often try to keep families together when convenient, but their financial interests all too often overrode any humanitarian concern.

In the areas of religion, folk beliefs, and cultural life, blacks were, in general, able to preserve sufficient autonomy to provide a distinctively African input into what was to become African-American culture, while also exercising a considerable and still growing influence over American culture more generally. Slave masters, once they were reconciled to the idea of slaves becoming Christians at all, sought to control and restrict access to those preachers

Above: Armed slaves battle with a band of slave catchers.

Right: Nat Turner, leader of a slave uprising which claimed the lives of more than fifty whites before his capture, illustrated here.

Right: The mathematician Benjamin Banneker (1731-1806), disputed Jefferson's claims of black intellectual inferiority, and in 1789 served on the commission planning the layout of Washington D.C.

Below right: Benjamin Banneker's *Almanac*, published annually from 1792 to 1802.

who would uphold the status quo. Slaves listened to many sermons on the theme of obedience to the masters in all things. In the ante-bellum South the Baptists, Methodists, and Presbyterians, acting on the urging of wealthy planters mostly moved away from even their earlier limited opposition to aspects of slavery. Their support for segregated congregations, and to a lesser extent for black preachers, did, however, provide a space in which the spiritual concerns and more vocal worship of the black community, both slave and free, could find expression. In public services the black preachers had to be careful to confine their comments to spiritual matters, but in the night time prayer meetings held in a secluded spot on the plantations they were free to sermonize on the bible's teaching regarding justice, equality, and the prospects of a brighter world to come on earth as well as in heaven. The Baptist church was particularly popular among the black population of the South, but it was a Baptist worship that took on new forms as a black church, catering to the qualities of religiosity Genovese aptly summarized as "this pride, this self respect, this astonishing confidence in their own spiritual quality."

If the closer interaction with the larger white community prevented the development of Afro-Caribbean religions of the type that flourished in slave societies elsewhere in the Americas, it has long been clear from the work of scholars from Zora Neale Hurston onwards that the folk beliefs of the black South, influenced as they were by many similar European-originated beliefs in potions, soothsayers, and spells held by the poorly educated whites, nevertheless contained a solid core of African-derived ideas and practices. Voodoo, conjurers, and conjure women, the use of grave dirt as a key ingredient in spells, threads to bind packets of "medicine," bottles to trap spirits, all had their sources in African cultures such as Kongo and Yoruba. Whites as well as blacks consulted African-born healers and conjurers in search of cures, fortune telling, and love potions. Music also explored deep African continuities, from ring-shouts and field-hollers, to the blues and jazz. A slave drum collected in Virginia in the late seventeenth century and now in the British Museum, London, is entirely African in form.

Throughout the ante-bellum era several Southern states passed laws that increasingly restricted the rights of

BANNEKER's
ALMANACK
AND
EPHEMERIS
FOR THE
YEAR OF OUR LORD 1793
BEING
THE FIRST AFTER BISSEXTILE OR LEAP-YEAR
CONTAINING
THE MOTIONS OF THE SUN AND MOON;
THE TRUE PLACES AND ASPECTS OF THE PLANETS;
THE RISING AND SETTING OF THE SUN;
RISING, SETTING, AND SOUTHING OF THE MOON;
THE LUNATIONS, CONJUNCTIONS, AND ECLIPSES;
AND
THE RISING, SETTING, AND SOUTHING OF THE PLANETS AND NOTED FIXED STARS.

PHILADELPHIA:
PRINTED AND SOLD BY *JOSEPH CRUKSHANK*, NO. 87, HIGH-STREET.

Running Away

The naturalist John James Audubon discovered a runaway hiding in the Louisiana swamps in the late 1820s.

"A stentorial voice commanded me to 'stand still, or die' . . . Presently a tall firmly-built negro emerged from the bushy underwood . . . 'Master,' said he, 'I am a runaway . . . My camp is close by, and as I know you cannot reach home this night, if you will follow me there, depend upon my honour you shall be safe until the morning.'

"There, in the heart of the cane-brake, I found a regular camp . . . The wife raised not her eyes towards mine, and the little ones, three in number, retired into a corner . . . The Runaway told me a tale of which the following is the substance.

"About 18 months before, a planter residing not very far off, having met with some losses was obliged to expose his slaves at a public sale . . . The Runaway chanced to be purchased by the overseer of the plantation; the wife was bought by an individual residing about a hundred miles off; and the children went to different places along the river . . .

"On a stormy night . . . the poor negro made his escape, and . . . made directly for the cane brake, in the centre of which I found his camp. A few nights afterwards he gained the abode of his wife, and the very next after their meeting, he led her away. The children one after another he succeeded in stealing . . . I promised to accompany them to the plantation of their first master. We soon reached the plantation . . . Ere an hour had elapsed, the Runaway and his family were looked upon as his own. He afterwards repurchased them from their owners."

Below: Local poor whites were recruited by slaveholders throughout the South to mount patrols and hunt for fugitives. Their brutality, often directed as much at free blacks and slaves as fugitives, made them hated and feared.

Above: The slave quarters on a Southern plantation.

slave-holders to manumit, or free, their slaves. This action was primarily taken in response to concerns expressed by both the planters and poor whites about the growing number of free blacks. In the years before 1810 the free black population in the South had grown quite rapidly. In Virginia for example, according to the historian Peter Kolchin, the proportion of free people among the black population rose from under one percent in 1782, to 4.2 percent in 1790, and 7.2 percent—amounting to a total of some 30,570—by 1810. Some of these were able to earn sufficient money to purchase freedom for themselves and their close family, while many others were freed by the masters out of idealism in the years immediately after the Revolution. Still others were selectively freed, as a favorite, a mistress, or a child of a slave-holder.

The majority of these free blacks were in the North, and in the upper states of the South, where some ten percent of blacks were free in 1810, while in the deep South states less than two percent had been freed. Even in the North free blacks were subject to discrimination and mostly confined to menial occupations, often prevented from voting, and restricted in their movements across state lines. Free blacks in the South lived largely in the towns and cities, particularly in Washington D.C. and Baltimore, where many worked in factories, as domestic servants, or as artisans. In the rural areas they were small scale farmers, casual laborers or craftsmen. In the deep South, however, in Louisiana and South Carolina, there was a small and unrepresentative number of free blacks, mostly of mulatto or mixed race origins, who occupied many skilled positions, and in a minority of cases, owned substantial wealth. Many of these were the descendants of families of French and Spanish colonists who looked on themselves as among the social elite of towns such as Charleston and New Orleans. Like other wealthy people at the time, these free blacks were themselves often slave owners. Genovese notes that the wealthiest of them was August Dubuclet of Iberville Parish, who had ninety-four slaves on a plantation of over 1,200 acres. In the years before the Civil War, and particularly after the passage of the Fugitive Slave Act in 1850 strengthened the laws which allowed escaped slaves to be returned to their owners in the South, life for all free blacks became still more difficult as white hostility and the dangers of re-enslavement increased.

5 The Road to Freedom: Abolition in Britain

Although some of the first public support for the abolition of slavery came from American Quakers, it was in Britain that the decisive developments, which would ultimately lead to abolition throughout the Atlantic, took place. In the 1750s Britain was the dominant economic and maritime power of the western world. The transatlantic slave trade was expanding annually in a vain effort to meet the insatiable demands for labor in the New World. Britain had the major share of this trade, with ships from Bristol and Liverpool carrying tens of thousands of Africans each year to the Americas. Britain's own suger plantation colonies of the Caribbean flourished. Slavery seemed securely estab-

lished as one of the cornerstones of a period of unprecedented economic prosperity. Only the most radical and apparently eccentric voiced public criticisms. Yet within sixty years Britain would pass laws ending the slave trade in all her colonies. Both diplomatic and military action throughout the nineteenth century would become focused on the further goal of persuading or compelling other nations to follow the same path. The world's biggest slave trading nation was to become the prime mover behind the ultimately successful suppression of the trade.

The reasons for this dramatic shift in policy were varied and complex. Although Britain's commercial rivals in France and America were, from the start, suspicious that the underlying motivation was to weaken their own economies and interfere with their shipping, in Britain itself it was widely accepted that pure altruism lay behind the change towards abolition. It was seen, in numerous historical accounts of the abolition movement that were written in the nineteenth century and first half of the twentieth century, as the triumph of good over evil. The abolitionists, inspired by humanitarian interest in the welfare of Africans and backed up by the forces of a new economic liberalism, had out-argued and outvoted the reactionary forces of the sugar lobby; the absentee planters, and the slave traders of Liverpool and Bristol. Recognizing that this was the morally right policy, successive British

Left: **William Wilberforce became the spokesman and leader of the abolitionists in the British Parliament in 1787, taking advantage of his friendship with the Prime Minister, William Pitt to promote their cause.**

Right: **The poet Alexander Pope (1688–1744) was among the early critics of slavery, drawing attention to its inconsistency with the belief in human dignity and the rights of man promoted by the new Enlightenment philosophy.**

Left: The Lord Justice, Lord Mansfield, reluctantly advanced the cause of abolition in England when he ruled on June 22, 1772, in a case brought by Granville Sharp, that there was no positive support for slavery in English law. The outrage caused a decade later by his 1783 ruling in the notorious *Zong* case that slaves were legal jettison as if they were horses, served to rally public support for abolition.

supposed economic pressures and the actual timing and procedures of parliamentary and legal action against slavery. The view of Williams and his followers that abolition was a response to the declining economic significance of the West Indies and of slave-carrying in British trade has been refuted by more recent research demonstrating that this decline occurred after—not before—1807. Attention has therefore shifted back towards more nuanced accounts of the abolitionist movement and the intellectual climate it helped create.

Sporadic attacks on the morality of slave trading were made even as Britain was entering the trade on a significant scale. In 1665 Richard Baxter argued that those who:

"catch up poor Negroes, or people of another land, that never forfeited life or liberty, and to make them slaves, and sell them, . . . one of the worst kinds of thefts in the world, and such persons are to be taken as the common enemies of mankind."

Such voices were, however, rare and of no significant influence. It was not until the following century that the broad-based opening up of intellectual life, known today as the Enlightenment, began to provide an arena for a more sustained and effective critique of slavery. Even then however, although it was criticized by such eminent public figures as John Locke and Alexander Pope, and

governments had then acted to enforce it world-wide as the slave trading era gave way to a new and more far reaching period of Imperialism. It was only with the decline of the British Empire in the aftermath of World War II that new voices were heard arguing that this picture was unduly complacent and self-serving. In his pioneering book *Capitalism and Slavery* (1944), Eric Williams suggested that the importance of the humanitarian motive had been greatly exaggerated. Instead, he argued, Pitt, the British Prime Minister, supported the abolition bills primarily out of a concern to shore up Britain's own competitive position in the sugar industry and undermine that of her French and Spanish rivals. British sugar-producing islands in the West Indies were, unlike Cuba and those still retained by the French after the loss of Saint-Domingue, well stocked with slaves already. Britain had alternative, and potentially more competitive, sources of sugar in the East Indies. By 1807, against the background of the Napoleonic wars, there was an overproduction of sugar in British colonies. Britain, he claimed, acted to abolish the slave trade because it suited the economic interests of the day.

Although Williams' account was a useful reminder of the economic background of abolition, specific aspects of his analysis have been heavily criticized, in particular his suggestion that a glut of sugar existed. More fundamentally, he failed to demonstrate any clear link between the

Right: John Wesley (1703–1791), founder of the Methodist Church, spoke out repeatedly against slavery. Methodists and other nonconformist Christians were to be crucial in both the leadership and the mass following of the Abolitionist cause in Britain and the United States.

Left: A captured slave schooner that was bound for Cuba with 320 slaves still alive on board, when it was deliberately run aground on the coast of Jamaica after being pursued by *H.M.S. Arab*, 1857.

awareness of the brutalities of slave life was increasingly widespread in intellectual and political circles, few considered seriously the prospect of abolition. The Evangelical revival that spread throughout England in the mid-eighteenth century, with its emphasis on the study of the Bible and the spread of working class literacy that it promoted under the leadership of John Wesley and the Methodist Church, was of crucial importance. Wesley was a vociferous and uncompromising opponent of slavery, castigating it as a fundamental source of injustice and cruelty. While the Quakers were important in the leadership of the abolition movement, it was the efforts of Methodists and other nonconformist churches that provided the mass support for abolition in Britain throughout the following decades. A further dimension was added to the religious and humanitarian critique of slavery with the growing feeling that it was an outmoded and economically inefficient method of labor organization. This radical view found its most influential support with the publication, in 1776, of Adam Smith's classic text of market economics, *The Wealth of Nations*.

The first moves towards the organization of an abolition movement in Britain began with efforts to alter the legal position of blacks on British soil. Although there was no labor demand for African slaves in Britain, many of the wealthy absentee landlords of West Indian sugar plantations had brought favored slaves to work as domestic servants in their town houses and country estates. By the 1770s there were some 15,000 such slaves in Britain, together with a smaller number of mostly impoverished free blacks concentrated in London and other port cities. In 1765 Granville Sharp, a junior civil servant, came across a fugitive slave, called Jonathan Strong, stumbling beaten and almost blind in a London street. Together with his brother, who was a doctor, Sharp took the man in and nursed him back to health. However, two years later, the owner, a lawyer from Barbados by the name of Lisle, discovered that his slave had survived and arranged to have him kidnapped and sold to a West Indian planter. Before he could be exported Sharp filed a petition for assault against Lisle, which the slave owner countered by issuing a writ accusing Sharp of stealing his property. Although Lisle backed

The *Zong* Atrocity

Granville Sharp, the pioneering British abolitionist, wrote the following account of the notorious *Zong* incident.

"19 March 1783, Gustavus Vassa called on me with an account of 132 Negroes being thrown alive into the sea, from on board an English slave-ship.

"The circumstances of this case could not fail to excite a deep interest. The master of a slave-ship trading from Africa to Jamaica, and having 440 slaves on board, had thought fit, on a pretext that he might be distressed on his voyage for want of water, to lessen the consumption of it in the vessel, by throwing overboard 132 of the most sickly among the slaves. On his return to England, the owners of the ship claimed from the insurers the full value of those drowned slaves, on the ground that there was an absolute necessity for throwing them into the sea, in order to save the remaining crew, and the ship itself The underwriters contested the existence of the alleged necessity; or, if it had existed, attributed it to the ignorance and improper conduct of the master of the vessel. This contest of pecuniary interest brought to light a scene of horrid brutality which had been acted during the execution of the detestable plot. From the trial it appeared that the ship *Zong*, Luke Collingwood master, sailed from the island of St Thomas, on the coast of Africa, 6 September 1781 with 440 slaves and 14 whites on board, for Jamaica,

and that in the November following she fell in with that island; but instead of proceeding to some port, the master, mistaking, as he alleges, Jamaica for Hispaniola, ran her to leeward. Sickness and mortality had by this time taken place on board the crowded vessel: so that, between the time of leaving the coast of Africa and the 29th of November, sixty slaves and seven white people had died; and a great number of the surviving slaves were then sick and not likely to live. On that day the master of the ship called together a few of the officers, and stated to them, that, if the sick slaves died the natural death, the loss would fall on the owners of the ship; but, if they were thrown alive into the sea, on any sufficient pretext of necessity for the safety of the ship, it would be the loss of the underwriters, alleging, at the same time, that it would be less cruel to throw sick wretches into the sea, than to suffer them to linger out a few days under the disorder with which they were afflicted.

"To this inhuman proposal the mate, James Kelsal, at first objected; but Collingwood at length prevailed on the crew to listen to it. He then chose out from the cargo 232 slaves, and brought them on deck, all or most of whom were sickly, and not likely to recover, and he ordered the crew by turns to throw them into the sea. 'A parcel' of them were accordingly thrown overboard, and, on a second counting on the succeeding day, was proved to have amounted to forty-two.

Right: Granville Sharp brought a case before the Lord Justice, Lord Mansfield, in which he ruled that there was no positive support for slavery in English law. The Lord Justice would, however, cause outrage a decade later by his 1783 ruling in the notorious *Zong* case that slaves were legal jettison.

"On the third day the remaining thirty-six were brought on deck, and, as these now resisted the cruel purpose of their masters, the arms of twenty-six were fettered with irons, and the savage crew proceeded with the diabolical work, casting them down to join their comrades of the former days. Outraged misery could endure no longer; the ten last victims sprang disdainfully from the grasp of their tyrants, defied their power, and leaping into the sea, felt a momentary triumph in the embrace of death."

The court case that followed underlined the cynicism of English law at the time, which was summarized by an insurance lawyer in 1781 as follows:

"The insurer takes upon him the risk of the loss, capture, and death of slaves, or any other unavoidable accident to them; but natural death is always understood to be expected: —by natural death is meant, not only when it happens by disease or sickness, but also when the captive destroys himself through despair, which often happens; but when slaves are killed . . . to quell an insurrection . . . then the insurers must answer."

The owners of the *Zong* claimed from the insurers the full value of the murdered slaves—£30 a piece—on the grounds that there was an absolute necessity to throw them into the sea in order to save the remaining crew. The necessity given was scarcity of water. As it turned out, there was no lack of water. When the first "parcel" of slaves was thrown overboard, no one in the ship, white or black, had been on short allowance. The ship arrived in Jamaica on 22 December with 420 gallons to spare. The "absolute necessity" was in fact Collingwood's avarice. If the disease-ridden slaves died, there would be no insurance forthcoming and Collingwood's commission would be forfeit.

What horrified Sharpe was that the law concerned itself only with the narrow question of whether Collingwood had acted out of necessity or not. As the Solicitor-General, John Lee, for the owners, brutally put it:

"What is all this vast declamation of human people being thrown overboard? The question after all is; was it voluntary, or an act of necessity? This is a case of chattels or goods. It is really so: it is the case of throwing over goods; for to this purpose of the insurance, they are goods and property: whether right or wrong, we have nothing to do with it. This property . . . (has) been thrown overboard: whether or not for the preservation of the rest, that is the real question."

At one point in the course of his tirade Lee, turning to Granville Sharpe, who attended all the hearings, was even more vulgar. He exclaimed somewhat violently to the judges, that:

"A person was in Court (at the same time turning round and looking at me) who intended to bring on a criminal prosecution for murder against the parties concerned: but,' said he, 'it would be madness: the Blacks were property . . . If any man of them was allowed to be tried at the old Bailey for murder, I cannot help thinking, if that charge of murder was attempted to be sustained, it would be folly and rashness to a degree of madness: and, so far from the charge of murder lying against these people, there is not the least imputation—of cruelty I will not say, but—of impropriety: not in the least!!!"

As a result of the *Zong* case, no one who examined the evidence could deny the injustices either of the trade itself or of English law. Although the owner won the case, the judgement was overturned on appeal.

Below: An 1833 print showing slaves being thrown overboard to avoid a British naval patrol combating the illicit trade. Ships captured with slaves on board were liable to confiscation.

down in response to public outrage before any legal ruling took place, this public concern was itself evidence that the tide of popular opinion in Britain was running against the planters. A second case brought by Sharp on behalf of another fugitive ended inconclusively, with the Lord Chief Justice, Lord Mansfield, reluctant to do anything which might offend either the planters or the London public. A more decisive outcome had to await the action taken by Sharp on behalf of a third fugitive, James Somersett, in 1772. This case was to become a landmark judgement in British legal history, although it did not, as some abolitionists claimed at the time, and some accounts have subsequently argued, in itself result in the legal abolition of slavery in Britain. Despite considerable prevarication and reluctance, the Lord Chief Justice finally ruled on June 22, that since there was no positive endorsement of slavery in British law, it could not be upheld through the courts. The ownership rights claimed by the master under the law of the colony of Virginia could not override British common law presumptions in favor of the liberty of   individuals. However, while this was a major setback for slave-holders and seriously challenged their ability to flaunt their slaves in their mother country, it did not directly liberate the slaves already in Britain, it merely prevented them being returned forcibly to the Indies.

In the years after 1772 concern with the abolition of the slave trade went from being the preoccupation of a vocal minority to a major focus of public interest. The organization of this upsurge in abolitionism was greatly assisted by widespread outrage at the outcome of the notorious *Zong* incident of 1783. The courts upheld a claim for reimbursement brought after the captain of the slave ship *Zong*, allegedly suffering from an epidemic and a shortage of water, had 132 sick slaves thrown into the sea, hoping to recoup his losses through a claim from the insurers. The Lord Chief Justice's ruling that in law the owners were as entitled to compensation as if horses had been jettisoned brought home to a wide public the nature of the Middle Passage. In response to this case six prominent Quakers formed a committee to promote "the relief and liberation of the Negro slaves in the West Indies and for the discouragement of the Slave Trade on the coast

Below: A large group of Africans at Fort Augusta, Jamaica, after being rescued from a slave ship by a British destroyer in 1857.

Right: A cartoon of 1833 satirizing the Duke of Wellington's opposition to the Abolition Bill. Both pro and anti-slavery factions made use of newspapers, cartoons, and pamphlets to argue their cause.

Below right: A well-known painting depicting Thomas Clarkson addressing the important anti-slavery convention at Freemason Hall, London, in 1840.

of Africa." Granville Sharp, along with Thomas Clarkson and Josiah Wedgwood, the leading pioneer of the industrial production of pottery, founded the "Society for the Abolition of the Slave Trade." In 1787, Wedgwood designed and widely distributed some 200,000 copies of a pottery seal for the society, whose motif was a kneeling enchained African, with the words "Am I not a man and a brother?" Clarkson gathered a huge dossier detailing the procedures and abuses of the trade, which was to provide valuable ammunition as the dispute with the planters and their apologists became more bitter.

William Wilberforce, a well connected young member of Parliament, was persuaded by Clarkson in 1787 to become the leader of a parliamentary assault on slavery. It was his influence with leading political figures that led the Prime Minister to appoint a Committee of the Privy Council to investigate the slave trade the following year.

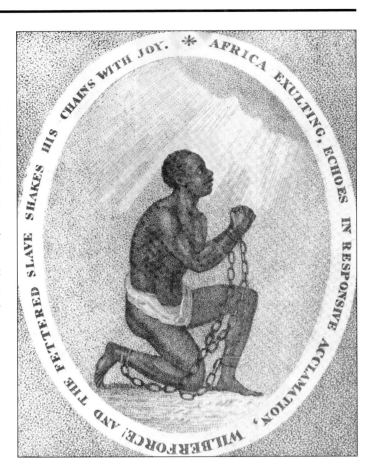

Right: This image of a kneeling and enchained slave raising his face towards the sunlight of emancipation was the key theme of Abolitionist propaganda in Britain, reproduced in numerous different forms on prints, medals, plates and other ephemera.

Below: The great Anti-Slavery Meeting in Exeter Hall, London, in 1841.

Buxton, Crusader for Human Rights

Thomas Fowell Buxton, who succeeded Wilberforce as Britain's leading Abolitionist, was a persuasive advocate for the humanitarian benefits of Britain's campaign against slavery:

"I am not so sanguine as to suppose that we can at once, by a single effort, solve the problem which lies before us. The deliverance of Africa will put our patience and perseverance to no ordinary trial. We must deliberately make up our minds to large and long-continued expense, to persevering labours, and to serve disappointments. I wish not in any degree to conceal from myself; or from others, these truths.

"But the question is,—Shall such an experiment be made? There are two mighty arguments which

should prompt us to such an undertaking: the intense miseries of Africa, and the peculiar blessings which have been showered upon this country by the mercy of Divine Providency. With regard to the first, I need not again plunge into the sickening details of the horrors which accompany this bloody trade, and of the sanguinary rites, which there bear the name of religion. Whether we look to the vast space which is there made a theatre of public misery, or calculate how many deeds of cruelty and carnage must be perpetrated every day in the year, in order to make up the surprising total documents, we know to be realized, there is enough to awaken the deepest pity and to arouse the most energetic resolution.

"Turning to the second consideration, we cannot fail to see how signally this nation has been preserved, and led forward to an extent of power and prosperity, beyond what almost any other nation has been permitted to reach . . .

"I believe that Great Britain can, if she will, under the favour of the Almighty, confer a blessing on the human race. It may be that at her bidding a thousand nations now steeped in wretchedness, in brutal ignorance, in devouring superstition, possessing by the one trade, and that one the foulest evil that domestic peace, shall, under British tuition, emerge from their debasement, enjoy a long line of blessings—education, agriculture, commerce, peace, industry, and the wealth that springs from it; and, far above all, shall willingly receive that religion which, while it confers innumerable temporal blessings, opens the way to an eternal futurity of happiness."

Left: The English reformer William Wilberforce 1759–1833.

Clarkson was able to lay much of his evidence before this committee, persuading them that, in spite of the rosy picture of slavery presented by the planters' supporters, they should recommend the subject for a full debate. The efforts of the abolitionist movement to mobilize popular sentiment through public meetings and the distribution of anti-slavery pamphlets and prints bore fruit in a deluge of petitions to Parliament from all regions of the country. Women played a particularly prominent role in the organization of popular opposition to slavery. Nevertheless, in Parliament the debate had to be postponed because of Wilberforce's poor health, and when the motion in favour of abolition was moved it failed by a majority of 163 votes to 88, benefiting from the deep purse of the sugar lobby.

The following year, however, when the issue was returned, the weight of public concern was reflected in the passage of a resolution by the House of Commons calling for the total abolition of the trade. The second chamber of Parliament, the House of Lords, was a major obstacle to change, acting to delay the bill's further progress and to

defeat a subsequent bill that proposed to abolish "the supply by British merchants of slaves to foreign settlements." Continued delay seemed likely as the pro-slavery camp was boosted by reaction to the excesses of egalitarianism in revolutionary France. The outbreak of war with France at first promised still further delay, but in its aftermath, with British forces in control of French and Dutch colonies in the Caribbean, and the example of the massacre of whites in Saint-Domingue showing the apparent risks of inaction, members of both Houses of Parliament were more receptive. A coalition government lead by the pro-abolitionists Grenville and Fox was formed in 1806. The same year a partial Abolition Bill was finally passed, prohibiting the sale of slaves to foreign lands or their importation into the newly gained colonies in the Caribbean. The following year saw the passage of a more sweeping measure under which from January 1, 1808, "all manner of dealing and trading in slaves" was "utterly abolished, prohibited and declared to be unlawful" throughout the British Empire. The penalties of a £100 fine and forfeiture of the vessel were quickly increased. In 1811 slave trading became a crime punishable by transportation or death.

The success of the abolitionists, remarkable though it was, was as yet only a limited one. The slaves in the British colonies of the Caribbean had not been set free and the other nations of Europe and the Americas were still

Below: An Abolitionist drawing by Cruikshank depicting a captain's cruel treatment of a female slave. Women played an important part in the campaign against slavery, and concern about the sexual exploitation of female slaves was frequently expressed.

Left: A set of slave chains brought home by the missionary David Livingstone to publicize the continuing plight of slaves in late nineteenth century East Africa.

Below: Rescued slaves on board a British warship. Most were landed at Freetown in Sierra Leone, where a missionary settlement had been established.

actively involved in the transatlantic trade. With regard to the existing slaves, at first Wilberforce's successor as leader of the movement, Thomas Fowell Buxton, hoped that cutting off the prospect of new slaves would lead the planters themselves to improve markedly the conditions of their workers out of self-interest. It soon became clear that this was not going to happen. An Anti-Slavery Society was established in 1823, and in response to continued popular pressure, the British government passed laws to reform slave conditions throughout the British West Indies. Among these was the abolition of the whip and of flogging female slaves, the freeing of all female children born after 1823, the granting of a day off for religious instruction, and a limit on the working day to nine hours. Instead of complying with these measures, the planters did all in their power to delay their enactment, provoking a series of major rebellions among slaves throughout the British colonies. The bloody suppression of these revolts,

Above: Berwick Street, Freetown, the capital of Sierra Leone pictured in 1880. Freetown was established as a refuge, at first in an unsuccessful attempt to provide a home for the impoverished free blacks of London, but subsequently for the many Africans freed from slave ships by British naval patrols.

the harsh reprisals taken against captured rebels and their sympathisers in the colonies, particularly the hanging of forty-seven slaves in Demerara in 1823, and the execution of 100 more in Jamaica in 1832, outraged public opinion in Britain. Helped by the influx of new members of parliament following the extension of the franchise in the Reform Bill, decisive action was finally taken. The Bill for the Abolition of Slavery became law on the August 29, 1833. The continued influence of the planters was, however, marked by the granting of £20 million in compensation for the loss of their "property" and the requirement that the freedmen be obliged to serve a further seven years as apprentices.

Eager to take effective steps to limit the trade still carried on by the other maritime powers, during the early years of the nineteenth century Britain was able to use the rights of search and seizure—in force during the continuing Napoleonic wars—to harass any slavers intercepted off the African coast. The dubious legal basis for some of these actions, however, added to the suspicion and scepticism with which the authorities of France, Portugal, Spain, and America regarded the British conversion to the humanitarian cause. When peace returned, the question of restricting or abolishing the slave trade became inextricably bound up with issues of national pride, commercial rivalry, and maritime rights, greatly assisting the attempts by pro-slavery forces to delay any effective controls. In 1816, British attempts to draft an international treaty setting up a permanent bureau to effect abolition failed in the face of French and Russian opposition, and it became increasingly clear that the only way forward was to negotiate individual treaties with each of the main nations involved.

Under pressure from the British, in 1817 the Spanish signed a treaty under which they received £400,000 compensation in return for an agreement to outlaw trading by

Spanish nationals north of the equator with immediate effect, extending to below the line from 1820. The Portuguese agreed only to ban trading north of the equator. In order to enforce these treaties and to exercise the limited rights of search, they authorized a small squadron of ships to patrol the West African coast. Courts were set up under the joint jurisdiction of the treaty nations to decide the fate of captured vessels. However, even when they succeeded in capturing a slaver, no conviction could be obtained unless the ship was found to have slaves actually on board. Later modifications allowed ships demonstrably equipped for slaving to also be seized, but even this could be circumvented by measures to reduce the incriminating evidence.

France finally signed the first of a series of treaties in 1831 but continued opposition to British intervention with the free passage of French ships largely overrode the growing pro-abolitionist sentiment in the country. Eventually, it was alarm at the challenge to French commercial and imperial interests in Africa posed by the tactic

adopted by the British in the 1840s of signing anti-slavery treaties with local African rulers that prompted the French to send their own naval vessels to interdict slavers. Even then there is little evidence that this force made any serious efforts against the trade.

The British naval patrols captured 1,287 ships between 1825 and 1865, releasing in the region of 130,000 Africans, most of whom were set ashore in the colony at Freetown, Sierra Leone, originally established under the sponsorship of Granville Sharp, as a refuge for the free blacks of Britain. This was only a modest proportion of the total enslaved, and it was clear that the patrols alone would never suppress the trade. More progress was made in concluding treaties with slave importing countries and this succeeded in closing off the markets. By the 1850s Cuba was the only substantial remaining outlet, and much of the remaining trade was carried on by American-flagged ships. The outbreak of the Civil War allowed the British finally to agree a right of search with the American authorities and take action against this last vestige of the transatlantic trade.

Left: A version of the famous abolitionist image, which was reproduced on prints, medals, and plates manufactured by the pioneering industrialist and abolitionist Josiah Wedgewood.

6 Someday We'll All Be Free: the Civil War and Abolition in America

Although abolitionist attacks on the morality of slavery had been made almost from the earliest days of colonization in America, it was in the years after independence that the issue of the future of slavery moved to take up center stage as the defining issue of national politics. The hopes for an end to slavery raised during the Revolutionary War had proved false and the dramatic expansion of cotton production had instead generated a huge increase in the number of people held as slaves throughout the American South. The split between the slave-holding Southern states and the increasingly hostile North widened over the course of the early decades of the nineteenth century as disputes arose over the admission of new states to the Union and over slave-holders attempts to recapture fugitives. The emergence of an organized Abolition movement in the North, uniting both blacks and whites in an often bitter struggle, was to be a key factor in keeping the issue at the forefront of public attention and mobilizing support to push for new measures in Congress.

Pro-slavery apologists in the South became increasingly extreme as their national and international isolation increased. The attempts at political compromise intended to hold the Union together in the face of these irreconcilable conflicts finally collapsed at the end of the 1860s with the attempted secession of the South. Although the resulting Civil War was fought primarily to restore the Union, it rapidly became apparent that victory for the Union forces would involve the ending of slavery and a

Right: American statesman and the sixteenth President of the United States, Abraham Lincoln (1809–1865), adopted a pragmatic approach to the politics of slavery in the early stages of the Civil War before recognizing the need for abolition.

Left: William Lloyd Garrison (1805–1879), radical proponent of abolition, founded the influential anti-slavery journal, *The Liberator*, in Boston in 1831.

victory for the Abolitionists. Black soldiers, recruited in their tens of thousands, played a key role in that victory.

The Abolition Movement

Quakers in Pennsylvania were the first settlers in America to publicly oppose slavery. As early as 1688 a number of them printed "The Germantown Protest," which stated that: "Now, tho' they are black, we cannot conceive there is more liberty to have them slaves, as it is to have other white ones . . . And those who steal or rob men, and those who buy or purchase them, are they not all alike?" Such sentiments continued to be expressed in Quaker circles over the following century and had a degree of impact on the passage of laws restricting slave imports in Pennsylvania and Massachusetts, it was only in the years after Independence that an organized abolition movement developed more widely. It built on the opposition to slavery that had been expressed by many of the leading figures of the Revolution and was assisted by the growing harassment of anti-slavery activists throughout the South. The movement brought moral and intellectual opposition to slavery together with the opposition of those who had suffered and continued to suffer its impact. Blacks were not, as pro-slavery apologists had argued, reconciled to and even happy in their lot as slaves. Rather, it was black hostility to slavery that laid the foundations for abolition. The historian Herbert Aptheker has called African-Americans "the first and most lasting abolitionists" arguing that "their conspiracies and insurrections, individual struggles, systematic flights, maroon communities, efforts to buy freedom, cultural solidarity, creation of anti-slavery organizations and publications—all preceded the black-white united efforts."

The abolition movement was the first modern mass campaign to be organized in America, and it involved the mobilization of both workers and intellectuals, men and women, blacks and whites, on a national scale. The American Anti-Slavery Society, founded in 1833, brought together abolitionists from New England, where William Lloyd Garrison was the most prominent activist, with those from Philadelphia, and from the newly opened up states of the Midwest. It was the pinnacle of a network of more than a thousand societies: the regional such as the "New England Anti-Slavery Society;" state organizations in New York, Rhode Island, Massachusetts, Ohio, and Pennsylvania; city groups in Boston, Providence and elsewhere; women's societies, of which the Boston and Philadelphia Female Anti-Slavery societies were prominent; youth groups; college societies; and denominational religious bodies.

Below: Title block of Garrison's *The Liberator*.

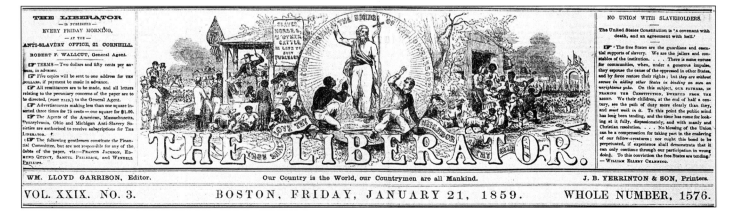

Left: American feminist, abolitionist, and reformer, Julia Ward Howe (1819–1910). She is best known for writing the *Battle Hymn of the Republic*. Engraving after a drawing by Porter.

Right: Harriet Beecher-Stowe, American anti-slavery author of, amongst other books, *Uncle Tom's Cabin*. She is pictured with a group of anti-slavery workers.

A key aspect of the work of many of these groups was to publicize the cause through the printing and distribution of pamphlets, books, and newspapers and to raise funds to continue these efforts. *The Liberator*, edited by William Lloyd Garrison and published in Boston from 1831 to 1865, was perhaps the most influential and effective of the regular newspapers, but others included *The Philanthropist* in Cincinnati, and *The Anti-Slavery Standard* in New York. Although the circulation of all these journals was quite limited, they were widely read and their articles frequently cited or reproduced in more mainstream publications.

Pamphlets and books, which had to be clandestinely distributed in the South at considerable personal risk, were read in their thousands throughout the country. The opinions of prominent abolitionists such as Wendell Phillips, Frederick Douglass and Angelina Grimke Weld were circulated through pamphlets to hundreds of thousands of readers. Harriet Beecher Stowe's *Uncle Tom's Cabin*, read by millions world-wide, is only the best known of many anti-slavery books published at this period. Frederick Douglass was born a slave in Maryland in 1817, but after a number of unsuccessful escape attempts succeeded in fleeing to Massachusetts in 1838. After an address to an anti-slavery

convention in Nantucket in 1841 revealed the eloquence of his public speaking he became one of the most prominent black members of the movement.

Forced to flee to Europe on two occasions to escape possible arrest, his speeches and writings, including his autobiography, first published in 1845 as *Narrative of the Life of Frederick Douglass, an American Slave*, were hugely influential. For many others, public lectures were also an important means of spreading the word, with long speaking-tours attracting hundreds, or even thousands, of listeners daily. Agents were hired to carry the message to more remote areas, often risking abuse and attacks. Women were prominent as activists in the movement and many abolitionists, from William Lloyd Garrison to Sojourner Truth, were also ardent supporters of women's rights. Truth (1797–1883), freed when slaves in New York State were emancipated in 1828, drew big crowds with her talks on both abolition and women's rights, while Garrison caused considerable controversy with his defence of the right of American women delegates to attend the "World Anti-Slavery Convention" in London in 1840.

Alongside this continuing propaganda campaign, the abolitionists took a number of more direct actions against slavery. These ranged from raising money in response to appeals from freedmen or women to help purchase their family members, through assisting fugitives, to John Brown's outright assault at Harper's Ferry. Many of the more radical abolitionists opposed the practice of paying slave-holders to sell people, but few were able to resist the often heartrending appeals made by freed mothers on behalf of children left behind in captivity.

The Fugitive Slave Law of 1793, allowed slave-holders to regain possession of any fugitives they could apprehend in the North. Although it became increasingly ineffective in the face of state personal liberty laws and often hostile public opinion, the presence of slave catchers was a constant threat to both fugitive slaves and free blacks. In 1850, as part of the deal with Southern states known as the Missouri Compromise (see page 135) a new law was passed strengthening these powers and obliging U.S. marshals to assist in the capture of fugitives. Members of the abolition movement played a vital role in sheltering runaway slaves and intervening where possible to prevent their return to slavery. Sometimes, as in 1854 when a Boston

The *Amistad* Affair

In late August 1839 rumors swept New York of a mysterious weatherbeaten ship that had been sighted at several points along the U.S. coastline over the previous few weeks. It was said that a band of Cuban slaves had killed the crew and were now roaming the Atlantic shores in search of provisions. On August 26, the United States survey brig *Washington* seized the vessel, the *Amistad,* and took her in tow to New London, Connecticut. In the struggle, the leader of the Africans jumped overboard to escape recapture and had to be forcibly returned to the ship. As Steven Spielberg's recent film *Amistad* has shown, a series of extraordinary events had led up to this incident, and the legal battle over the fate of the men, women, and children involved was to prove a vital rallying point for the cause of abolition in the United States.

The Africans were lead by a man named Sengbe Piah, a Mende-speaker from an area about ten days march inland from the coast of Sierra Leone. He had been captured in his home country and imported along with many others into Cuba in contravention of a treaty outlawing further slave imports signed by the Spanish in 1820. On June 26, 1839, he was among a total of 53 Africans, purchased at a slave auction in Havana, that were loaded aboard the *Amistad* for transport to the port of Puerto Principe. With them came two Cuban slave owners, Jose Ruiz, who had bought 49 of the captives for $400 each, and Pedro Montez, who purchased the four children. By

Right: John Quincy Adams, the sixth President of the United States, 1825. In retirement he played a key role in defending the African captives in the *Amistad* case.

Above: A contemporary newspaper illustration showing the death of Captain Ferrer.

June 30, Sengbe had managed to use a loose spike to undo the shackles confining the prisoners. Armed with cane knives found in a hold they attacked and killed the captain, Ramon Ferrer, and the ships cook Celestino. The two white crewmen escaped in a small boat, leaving the slavers Ruiz and Montez captive. Two of the Africans also died in the fight. Sengbe's hopes of leading his people back to freedom in Africa were thwarted by the deceit of the Cubans and the impact of a storm. For two months the vessel followed a zigzag course in U.S. waters. Rations were very short and eight more died from thirst and exposure before the ship was seized off New York.

From the start, the plight of the imprisoned Africans, who found themselves on trial for murder and piracy, attracted great public interest and sympathy, allowing abolitionists to raise contributions well beyond their normal range of sympathisers. Sengbe, who Ruiz had renamed Jose Cinque to support his argument that the men were legitimately held long-standing slaves not illegal new importees, became a hero in the sympathetic American press. The *New York Sun* reported: "had he lived in the days of Greece and Rome, his name would have been handed down to posterity as one who had practised those most sublime of all virtues—disinterested patriotism and unshrinking courage."

Over the following eighteen months the Africans were held captive while legal arguments raged over their future. The lawyers organized for them by the abolitionists had a sound enough case, namely that the Africans had clearly been imported illegally into Cuba and so were justified in their revolt. This was

accepted by the courts on January 13, 1840, but immediately appealed by the authorities. The administration, led by President Martin Van Buren, was anxious to avoid losing the support of pro-slavery Southern Democrats in the upcoming election, so was eager to find a way of complying with the demands of the slavers, supported by the diplomatic efforts of the Spanish Government, and return the Africans to Cuba. In anticipation of the Africans losing their case, the President had even sent a navy vessel to deport them to Cuba before an appeal could be made.

Aware of the need for an influential public figure to defend the Africans before the Supreme Court, the abolitionists persuaded the 73-year-old ex-President John Quincy Adams to come out of retirement and speak in court on their behalf On February 24, he addressed the court for over four hours presenting the key points of the defence. His eloquence and the evident justice of their cause carried the day and the Supreme Court set free the captives, ordering that they be allowed to return to Africa. Later that year, after funds had been raised and Sengbe and the leading campaigner had exchanged moving speeches at a farewell ceremony, the surviving thirty-five Africans set sail for home, accompanied by five American missionaries.

crowd tried unsuccessfully to rescue escapee Anthony Burns, obliging the government to send troops to escort the slave catchers on board a ship returning him to Virginia, this involved direct intervention, but equally often it required the financing of legal challenges.

An elaborate informal system of guides and refuges was developed to help fugitive slaves reach the British colony in Canada where they would be safe from any legal efforts to return them. This network, known as the Underground Railroad, helped conceal fugitives on isolated farms or provide them with the names of urban sympathizers where they could seek refuge for a few days before they could be guided to a suitable border crossing point such as Detroit or Buffalo. Even when slave-holders or their agents were not in direct pursuit, rewards were generally offered for their capture and fugitives had to be concealed or disguised to prevent their falling into the hands of professional or opportunist slave catchers. In some cases the organizers of the "Railroad" took the dangerous step of traveling far into the South themselves to assist escapees, risking imprisonment for slave-stealing or, especially if they were black, a real threat of lynching.

Harriet Tubman (c.1820–1913) was the best known of many who risked everything in this way. After reaching the North herself around 1849 she made a total of nineteen journeys from her home in Auburn, New York, to lead others, including her own parents, to freedom. In total Tubman, called the "Moses of her people," helped an estimated 300 people reach Canada.

Although earlier estimates that suggested tens of thousands benefited from the dedicated help of these selfless "conductors" were probably exaggerated, their contribution nevertheless extended far beyond the direct benefits to the individual men and women assisted. Each successful escape brought welcome publicity and a boost to the morale of the abolitionists while arousing further anger and bitterness among their opponents in the South. The more spectacular and newsworthy the escape the greater the benefit from the ensuing publicity. The case of Henry "Box" Brown was perhaps the most extraordinary of many dramatic escapades.

By the 1850s it was apparent to all that while the abolition movement had been successful in keeping the issue at the forefront of public attention the prospects for

Left: A former slave standing by a slave block in Fredericksburg, Virginia, on which slaves stood to be auctioned off to the highest bidder.

Right: American journalist, author, former slave, and leading abolitionist Frederick Douglass (1817–1895).

The Ordeal of Henry "Box" Brown

Henry Brown's audacious escape was perhaps the most dramatic of many incidents which provided much needed publicity to the abolitionists' cause:

"One day, while I was at work, and my thoughts were eagerly feasting upon the idea of freedom, the idea suddenly flashed across my mind of shutting myself up in a box, and getting myself conveyed as dry goods to a free state.

"Being now satisfied that this was the plan for me, I went to my friend Dr. Smith and having acquainted him with it, we agreed to have it put at once into execution . . .

"My next object was to procure a box, and with the assistance of a carpenter that was very soon accomplished, and taken to the place where the packing was to be performed. In the meantime, the store keeper had written to a friend in Philadelphia . . . It was deemed necessary that I should get permission to be absent from my work for a few days . . . I went off directly to the storekeeper who had by this time received an answer from his friend in Philadelphia . . . and had obtained permission to address the box to him . . . The box which I had procured was three feet one inch long, two feet six inches high, and two feet wide: and on the morning of the 29th of March, 1849, I went into the box—having previously bored three gimlet holes opposite my face, for air, and provided myself with a bladder of water . . . Being thus equipped for the battle of liberty, my friends nailed down the lid and had me conveyed to the Express Office . . .

"The next place we arrived at was the Potomac Creek, where the baggage had to be removed from the cars, to be put on board the steamer; where I was placed with my head down, and in this dreadful position had to remain nearly an hour and a half . . . I felt my eyes swelling as if they would burst from their

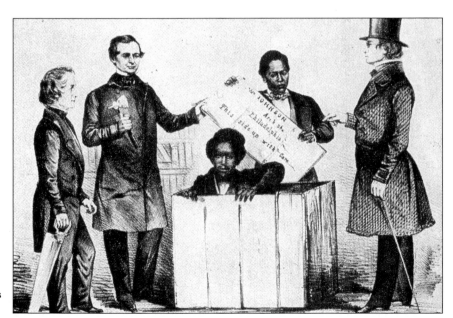

Right: Henry "Box" Brown arrives in Philadelphia.

sockets; and the veins on my temples were dreadfully distended with pressure of blood upon my head . . . I could hear a man saying to another, that he had travelled a long way and had been standing there two hours, and he would like to get somewhat to sit down; so perceiving my box, standing on end, he threw it down and then the two sat upon it. I was thus relieved from a state of agony which maybe more easily imagined than described. I heard one of them asking the other what he supposed the box contained; his companion replied he guessed it was 'THE MAIL.' I too thought it was a mail, but not such a mail as he supposed.

"The next place at which we arrived was the city of Washington, where I was taken from the steamboat, and again placed upon a waggon and carried to the depot right side up with care; but when the driver arrived at the depot I heard him call for some person to help to take the box off the waggon, and some one answered him to the effect that he might throw it off; but, says the driver, it is marked 'this side up with care; so if I throw it off I might break something.' The other answered him that it did not matter if he broke all that was in it, the railway company were able enough to pay for it. No sooner were these words spoken that I began to tumble from the waggon, and falling on the end where my head was, I could hear my neck give a crack, as if it had been snapped asunder and I was knocked completely insensible . . . I was then tumbled into the car with my head downward again, but the car had not proceeded far before, more luggage having to be taken in, my box got shifted about and so happened to turn up its right side; and in this position I remained till I got to Philadelphia . . .

"I was then placed on a waggon and conveyed to the house where my friend in Richmond had arranged I should be received. A number of persons soon collected round the box after it was taken in to the house, but as I did not know what was going on I kept myself quiet. I heard a man say 'let us rap on the box and see if he is alive,' and immediately a rap ensued and a voice said, tremblingly, 'Is all right within?' to which I replied—'all right.' The joy of the friends was very great; when they heard that I was alive they soon managed to break open the box, from the grave of slavery."

Above: The publicity generated by novel and successful escapes was a major boost to the abolitionist cause in America. One such case was that of Ellen Craft, a fugitive slave who came to England dressed as white man with her husband as her "slave."

real progress in the South were further away than ever. Harassment of free blacks and anti-slavery activists by both vigilante groups and legal restrictions in the region was increasing. The passage in 1850 of a strengthened Fugitive Slave Act had demonstrated that anti-slavery forces in Congress were prepared to make concessions in the face of Southern pressure. In this context abolitionists began to despair of peaceful means and moved towards more radical measures.

This was the context in which John Brown led what seemed to many to be a desperate and suicidal assault on the system. Although Brown has been portrayed by conservative historians as a fanatic and even a madman, his actions were informed by the recognition of the violence inherent in slavery and the ultimate necessity of using equally violent means to challenge it. He was not an isolated fanatic but a respected member of the movement and a close friend of Frederick Douglass, Harriet Tubman, and many other leading figures. While Douglass and others may have questioned the wisdom of his tactics at Harper's Ferry they recognized the rationale of his resort to force in

Above: Departure of African-Americans for Liberia, West Africa in 1838. Moves to encourage blacks to return to Africa were rejected by most black members of the abolition movement.

the attempt to rally opposition to slavery in a period of unprecedented national turmoil. W. E. B. Du Bois, writing in 1909, noted that "John Brown worked not simply for the Black Man—he worked with them, and he was a companion of their daily life, knew their faults and virtues, and felt, as few white Americans have felt, the bitter tragedy of their lot."

Brown, who was born in 1800, achieved nationwide notoriety when he led his five sons into Kansas to fight against bands of pro-slavery thugs who had murdered several abolitionists. In a fight at Pottawatomie Creek, on May 24, 1856, Brown and his sons avenged these murders by killing five of the terrorists, before successfully beating off a counter-attack a few months later by a larger party of

pro-slavery vigilantes from Missouri. Although Brown had long been considering a plan, discussed with colleagues such as Douglass, to form a band of armed resisters who could attack and harass pro-slavery forces from the shelter of the Allegheny Mountains, along the lines of guerrilla movements in the twentieth century, his attack, when it finally came on Saturday October 16, 1859, led to a fatal trap. With twenty-two followers armed with pikes and rifles, Brown seized control of the armoury at Harper's Ferry. A train which Brown allowed to pass through the town quickly spread the alarm and the rebels were surrounded by local militia reinforced by a company of Marines under Colonel Robert E. Lee. Ten of Brown's men, including two of his sons, were killed in the fighting that followed and by Monday the wounded Brown had been captured and charged with crimes including treason and murder. He was hanged forty days later. Despite the dismal failure of his attack the impact on the abolition movement and the climate of opinion in both the North and the South was electric. Brown's death was marked by

Above: Fugitive slaves. The vast majority of fugitives did not make the difficult break for the North, preferring to shelter near their homes and plantations.

Below: An anti-slavery meeting on Boston Common with free blacks in the crowd.

CAUTION!!

COLORED PEOPLE

OF BOSTON, ONE & ALL,

You are hereby respectfully CAUTIONED and advised, to avoid conversing with the

Watchmen and Police Officers
of Boston,

For since the recent ORDER OF THE MAYOR & ALDERMEN, they are empowered to act as

KIDNAPPERS

AND
Slave Catchers,

And they have already been actually employed in KIDNAPPING, CATCHING, AND KEEPING SLAVES. Therefore, if you value your LIBERTY, and the *Welfare of the Fugitives* among you, Shun them in every possible manner, as so many *HOUNDS* on the track of the most unfortunate of your race.

Keep a Sharp Look Out for KIDNAPPERS, and have TOP EYE open.

APRIL 24, 1851.

intense debate over the issue of slavery across Europe and America and he become the most famous martyr of the abolition campaign. As Du Bois commented, his time in prison and the debates provoked were "the mightiest abolition document that America has ever known."

Congress, Compromises, and the Abolition Struggle

The precarious mutual accommodation reached between pro- and anti-slavery interests in the immediate aftermath of the Revolution was threatened over the following decades by disputes over two major interrelated issues. The first was the status of free blacks in the North, and the impact upon them of both the attempts by slave owners to use the law to recover fugitives who had succeeded in escaping to non-slave states and of restrictions on the rights of free blacks to enter certain states. The second was the admission of new territories to the Union. These issues first came to a head in 1819 when Congress began to debate the admission of Missouri, taking on a particular intensity because the proposed new state threatened to upset the existing equilibrium of twenty states, ten of which were free and ten slave-holding. Missouri's state constitution not only provided for slavery but also barred

any immigration into Missouri of free blacks from other states. As abolitionists pointed out, this violated the article of the Constitution granting equal privileges and immunities to all citizens. Authorities as eminent as John Quincy Adams, then Secretary of State, felt that Northern states such as Massachusetts would be justified in passing retaliatory measures that similarly discriminated against citizens of Southern states, leading to a *de facto* dissolution of the Union. In the event, the so-called Missouri Compromise was reached, under which the state would be admitted along with its existing pro-slavery laws but slavery would be prohibited in further areas of the Louisiana Purchase territories north of latitude 36' 30". The admission of another slave state would be balanced by the simultaneous admission of Maine, which had previously been a part of Massachusetts.

The same issues resurfaced with even greater intensity thirty years later with the acquisition of vast new territories from Mexico following the Mexican-American War. Between August and September 1850, Congress passed a series of five measures, negotiated by Senator Henry Clay of Kentucky, which became known as the Compromise of 1850. The slave trade was abolished in the District of Columbia and the admission of California as a free state was approved. New Mexico and Utah were to be opened to settlement by both slave-holders and non-slavers, while Texas, already admitted as a slave state, was to be compensated for giving up claims to adjoining territory. Most controversially, the new and strengthened Fugitive Slave Act was passed, adding considerably to the bitterness

Left: Police notice to the "colored people of Boston" warning of the activities of slave catchers.

Below: Slave catchers kidnapping an escaped slave.

The Emancipation Proclamation

"Whereas, On the twenty-second day of September, in the year of our Lord one thousand eight hundred and sixty-two, a proclamation was issued by the President of the United States, containing, among other things, the following, to wit: 'That on the first day of January, in the year of our Lord one thousand eight hundred and sixty-three, all persons held as slaves within any State, or designated part of a State, the people whereof shall then be in rebellion against the United States, shall be then, thenceforward and forever, free, and the Executive Government of the United States, including the military and naval authority thereof; will recognise and act or acts to repress such persons, or any of them, in any effort they may make for their active freedom. That the Executive will, on the first day of January aforesaid, by proclamation, designate the States and respectively, shall then be in rebellion against the United States,

Below: Abraham Lincoln (1809–1865), president 1861–1865, at the signing of the Emancipation Proclamation which gave slaves their freedom.

and the fact that any State, and the people thereof, shall, on that day, be, in good faith, represented in the Congress of the United States, by members chosen thereto at elections, wherein a majority of the qualified voters of such state shall have participated, shall, in the absence of strong countervailing testimony, be deemed conclusive evidence that such State and the people thereof are not then in rebellion against the United States.'

"Now, therefore, I, Abraham Lincoln, President of the United States, by virtue of the power in me vested as Commander-in-Chief of the Army and Navy of the United States in time of actual armed rebellion against the authority and government of the United States, and as a fit and necessary war measure for suppressing the said rebellion, do, on this, the first day of January, in the year of our Lord one thousand eight hundred and sixty-three, and, in accordance with my purpose so do to, publicly proclaim for the full period of one hundred days from the day first above mentioned, order and designate as the States and parts of States wherein the people thereof respectively are this day in rebellion against the United States, the following, to wit: Arkansas, Texas, Louisiana (except the parishes of St. Bernard, Plaquemines, Jefferson, St. James, Ascension, Assumption, Terrebonne, Lafourche, St.Martin, and Orleans, including the city of New Orleans,) Mississippi, Alabama, Florida, Georgia, South Carolina, North Carolina, and Virginia (except the forty-eight counties designated as West Virginia, and also the counties of Berkley, Accomac, Northampton, Elizabeth City, York, Princess Ann, and Norfolk, including the cities of Norfolk and Portsmouth), and which excepted parts are for the present left precisely as if the proclamation were not issued.

"And, by virtue of the power and for the purpose aforesaid, I do order and declare that all persons held as slaves within the said designated States and parts of said States, are, and henceforward shall be, free; and that the Executive government of the United States, including the military and naval authorities thereof, will recognise and maintain the freedom of said persons.

"And I hereby enjoin upon the people so declared to be free, to abstain from all violence, unless in necessary self-defence, and I recommend to them that in all cases, when allowed, they labour faithfully for reasonable wages. And I further declare and make known, that such persons, of suitable condition, will be received into the armed service of the United States, to garrison forts, positions, stations and other places, and to man vessels of all sorts in the said service. And upon this act, sincerely believed to be an act of justice, warranted by the constitution, upon military necessity, I invoke the considerate judgement of mankind, and the gracious favour of Almighty God.

"In witness whereof I have hereunto set my hand, and caused the seal of the united States of be affixed (L.S.) Done at the city of Washington, this, the first day of January, in the year of our Lord one thousand eight hundred and sixty-three, and of the independence of the United States of America the eighty seventh."

A. Lincoln

of abolitionist disputes and arousing unprecedented popular support for fugitives in the North. The failure of these measures to diffuse the increasing hostility between North and South was emphasised by the forcing through by pro-slavery interests in 1854 of the Kansas-Nebraska Act, allowing settlers to formulate their own position on slavery thus breaching the 1920 Accords for the prohibition of slavery north of 36' 30". Disputes over this measure precipitated the final collapse of the Whig party and a re-alignment with anti-slavery Democrats from which the new Republican party emerged in July 1854. In 1857, a ruling finally emerged from the Supreme Court in the long-running Dred Scott case, arguing that the Missouri Compromise was unconstitutional since Congress lacked the power to prohibit slavery in any part of the Union.

Slavery became the issue around which the growing differences between the South and the remainder of the Union coalesced. The wider economic interests of the increasingly industrialized Northeast with its demand for protective tariffs, and the Congressional support for free

Above: Blacks in the North at the African Church, Cincinnati, Ohio.

Right: The publicity generated by the recapture of the escapee Anthony Burns in Boston 1854 was a *cause célèbre* for the abolition movement.

homesteads in the expanding territories to the West, came to seem increasingly at odds with the old-fashioned plantation economies of the South. Despite the passage of the Fugitive Slave Act, the ability of planters to enforce what they regarded as legitimate ownership rights over their "property" had been undermined by public opposition and the passage of personal liberty acts by state legislatures throughout the North. A split in the Democratic party along North-South lines in the 1860 Presidential election opened the way to election for the Republican nominee, Abraham Lincoln, on a platform of support for Northern economic interests and continued, if limited, opposition to slavery. Moves by Southern states to secede

THE ESCAPE ON SHIPBOARD.

ARREST IN BOSTON.

DEPARTURE FROM BOSTO

THE SALE.

THE ADDRESS.

THE PRISON.

Anthony Burns

from the Union followed rapidly and the long postponed confrontation began with the Southern attack on Fort Sumter in Charleston, South Carolina, on April 12, 1861.

The Civil War and Emancipation

The continued absence of any large-scale slave rebellions in the Confederate South allowed both conservative historians and nostalgic former slave-holders to perpetuate the false assertion that the majority of slaves were happy in their role and had made no effort to contribute to the Union cause. In fact however, as W. E. B. Du Bois pointed out in writing as early as 1835 of a slave "general strike," the wartime actions of a substantial proportion of the black people of the South were a major factor in the achievement of their own liberation. In this they were assisted not only by the wider strategic logic of the war situation, but also by the continued pressure on Lincoln and Congress from abolitionists, and by the action and example of black soldiers in the Union armies.

Despite the pivotal role played by the issue of slavery in

dividing the combatants and symbolizing the wider differences that had emerged between the Union and the Confederate South, the issue at stake from the outset was not the continuation or abolition of slavery but the preservation or break-up of the Union. In the early months of the war Lincoln repeatedly emphasized that the Republican Administration would not take any measures to outlaw slavery in existing slave states. This position was crucial to avoid alienating both important Northern Democrats and the key pro-Union slave states of Maryland, Delaware, Missouri, Kentucky, and the breakaway Unionist segment of Western Virginia. This pragmatic position remained Union policy for some time and it was only as the war dragged into an apparently prolonged stalemate in the latter part of 1862 that Lincoln's actions began to become more attuned to his personal opposition to slavery.

If there was no dramatic upsurge in outright rebellion among the slaves it is clear that many were able to keep reasonably informed about the progress of the war and take numerous minor individual acts of resistance and self-assertion. Taken together, these actions and attitudes both effectively weakened the Confederate war effort and sapped the already weakened confidence of the slave-holders in the future of their social system. The letters and journals of both men at the front and women at the plantation houses are full of evidence of an all-pervading anxiety over the continued loyalty of their most trusted slaves and the sense of betrayal felt when the extent of their own self-deceit over the true nature of paternalistic slave-holding could no longer be ignored.

Once the Union forces approached any district the pretence that master-slave relations were continuing as normal broke down, work in the fields and houses virtually ceased, and the flow of runaways to the Union lines became a flood. The issue of what to do with all these fugitives helped prompt a grudging reappraisal of policy by federal officials. At first some pro-slavery Union officers even allowed slave-holders to cross Union lines to reclaim their property, provoking outrage and internationally damaging publicity from abolitionists. In May 1861, however, Major-General Benjamin F. Butler in Virginia issued an order that fugitives were to be given employment and

AMERICAN
ANTI-SLAVERY
ALMANAC,
FOR
1840,

BEING BISSEXTILE OR LEAP-YEAR, AND THE 64TH OF AMERICAN INDEPENDENCE.   CALCULATED FOR NEW YORK; ADAPTED TO THE NORTHERN AND MIDDLE STATES.

NORTHERN HOSPITALITY—NEW YORK NINE MONTHS' LAW.
The slave steps out of the slave-state, and his chains fall.   A free state, with another chain, stands ready to re-enslave him.

Thus saith the Lord, Deliver him that is spoiled out of the hands of the oppressor.

NEW YORK:
PUBLISHED BY THE AMERICAN ANTI-SLAVERY SOCIETY,
NO. 143 NASSAU STREET.

Left: The *American Anti-Slavery Almanac* for 1840.

Above right: A recruitment poster urging blacks to join the Union Army.

Below right: The bombardment of Fort Sumter at the start of the Civil War.

COME AND JOIN US BROTHERS.

PUBLISHED BY THE SUPERVISORY COMMITTEE FOR RECRUITING COLORED REGIMENTS

The Fighting Refugees

In his book, *The Hallowed Ground,* Bruce Caffon left this moving account of the refugee crisis in the Union lines.

"A Union force came back to its base at Corinth, Mississippi, after some foray deeper into the state, and when it marched in it was followed by hundreds upon hundreds of fugitive slaves. The army command at Corinth did not want these people—had, in fact, very little idea what it could do with or about them—but it could not send them back, and it fenced off the big camp put the ex-slaves into it, detailed a couple of infantry regiments to guard it, and plucked a chaplain from the 27th Ohio and told him he was in charge. The soldiers objected bitterly to guard duty, declaring that they had come down to Dixie to fight Rebels and not to be policemen for a lot of runaway slaves, and the chaplain came up with an idea. Let him (he urged) form a few infantry companies from among the men in the contraband camp; with a little drill and the proper direction they ought to be able to stand guard . . .

"These contraband camps were not usually very inspiring places to look at. There was a huge one on a levee not far from Vicksburg, crammed with fugitives who huddled without shelter, subsisted on army rations, got no real care from anyone, and died by the dozen from bad sanitation, exposure, overcrowding, and general homesick bewilderment. yet the faith that had brought them here—a faith that freedom was good and that the road to it somehow led through the camps of the Union Army—did not seem to leave them, even a Wisconsin soldier who was detailed for duty around this camp looked on in silent wonder at the prayer meetings that were held every night. There were no lights; none was needed, he thought, since the leaders of the meeting had no Bibles or hymnals and could not have read from them if they had them; there was just a great crowd of men and women, dimly seen, bowed to the ground, swaying rhythmically as they prayed that God would set His people free and would send his blessing down on Massa Lincoln, Massa Grant, and all of Massa Lincoln's soldiers."

Below: A cartoon depicting escaped slaves, so-called "contrabrands."

effectively they became free. The second Confiscation Act of July 1862 made it an offence for any member of the armed forces to give up fugitive slaves. By this time, as the war progressed, the sheer numbers of runaways and refugees caused considerable logistical problems, with many people suffering real hardship in camps behind Union lines. As General Ulysses S. Grant advanced into Missouri, thousands of refugees almost swamped his often hostile troops. Some of these found work in the hospitals and kitchens of the army camps, or building trenches, while others worked as paid laborers in liberated areas.

The question of employing free blacks and escaped slaves in the ranks of the Union army also involved an often reluctant administration in a gradual accommodation with the realities of the war situation and the initiatives of large numbers of individual African-Americans who insisted on their right to serve. Racist prejudices ran deep in many parts of the army, and the remarks of General Thomas G. Stevenson made in the Sea Islands in 1863, that "he would rather have the Union forces defeated than win with Negro troops" were only an outspoken expression of quite widely held views. In the early months of the war attempts by both blacks and whites to organize black volunteer regiments were rejected, in part because it was feared that acceptance would have discouraged applications from white recruits. By the middle of 1862, however, attitudes were changing in the face of the continuing need for recruits as it became clear that the war would not be quickly resolved. Additionally, both the Northern media and many members of the Union Army reported back on the widespread assistance offered to the Union cause by slaves and free blacks, particularly in supplying valuable information about Confederate military positions.

The first large scale recruitment of blacks to the Union army was made—without explicit authorization by the pro-abolitionist General David Hunter—in the months of May and June 1862. In the South Georgia and Sea Islands area under his command, he began to organize and train a regiment of some 800 black soldiers. However, after intense debate in the newspapers and in Congress, the administration refused to grant the necessary authorization and the General was forced to disband the regiment in August. The precedent had been established, however, and later that same month the Secretary for War, Stanton, wrote to Brigadier General Rufus Saxton permitting him to

Above right: Senator Henry Clay of Kentucky, author of the 1850 compromise.

Right: General W. T. Sherman.

"arm, uniform and equip, and receive into the service of the United States such numbers of volunteers of African descent as you may deem expedient, not exceeding 5,000." A small unit from A Company of this regiment, the First South Carolina Volunteers, saw action in November 1862, after which their commanding officer reported that they "fought with astonishing coolness and bravery."

Throughout 1863, when black recruitment became much more widespread, a pattern emerged of white officers persistently deploying their African-American troops away from front line duties, using them wherever possible for heavy fatigue duties such as the construction of fortifications. Nevertheless, black soldiers inevitably became increasingly involved in actual fighting and the remaining prejudices about their military ability were at least gradually dispelled in the face of mounting evidence of their bravery in combat. Black soldiers, however, faced continuing discrimination from all sides. There were increasing complaints from both the soldiers and their white officers over the disparity in pay between black and

Left: John Brown (1800–1859), the American abolitionist. The song in memory of his exploits during the Harper's Ferry Raid, *John Brown's Body* **was a popular marching song with Union soldiers.**

Below: John Brown's Harper's Ferry Raid.

Right: John Brown going to his execution at Charlestown, Virginia.

Right: General Ulysses Simpson Grant (1822–1885), later the eighteenth President of the United States, at his headquarters at City Point during the American Civil War. He led the Union troops to victory.

Far right, top: Abraham Lincoln (1809–1865) making his inaugural address, surrounded by notables of the Civil War days.

Far right, below: Magee House in Canesto, New York was a staging post on the "Underground Railway," assisting fugitive slaves to escape to safety in Canada.

white recruits. In 1863 blacks received $10 per month less $3 clothing allowance, while whites got $13 plus $3.50 clothing allowance. It was not until the black soldiers of the Fifty-fourth and Fifty-fifth Massachusetts Regiments had refused all pay for many months, that pay was equalized. On the battlefield itself those who fell into the hands of the Confederates were frequently killed or re-enslaved. Throughout the war as a whole, despite the prejudice and hostility they encountered, some 180,000 African-Americans served in the Union Army, and a further 25,000 as sailors, doing much both to advance the cause of the United States forces and to at least mitigate some of the still widespread negative stereotypes.

At the same time as the Republican Administration was gradually changing its policy on the use of African-Americans in the Union army, Lincoln's pragmatic position on the wider issue of the future of slavery was also being supplanted by an increasingly pro-Abolitionist stance. Among the factors contributing to this were a response to a widening desire for more radical change among a growing sector of Northern public opinion and in the press, together with a desire to undermine international support for the Confederates. To come out decisively against slavery would make it impossible for Britain and France to continue their policy of official

Above right: A group of young black children sit amongst the ruins of Charleston, South Carolina, destroyed in fighting during the Civil War.

Right: Abraham Lincoln, making his famous "Gettysburg Address" speech at the dedication of the Gettysburg National Cemetery during the American Civil War. *Painting by Fletcher C Ransom U.S. Library of Congress.*

Far right: Robert E (Edward) Lee (1807–1870), one of the greatest of the Confederate generals in the Civil War.

neutrality and their attempts to take advantage of the rebellion to recover lost influence in the region. A series of measures were passed by Congress, beginning with the August 1861 Confiscation Act, effectively freeing any slaves used by their masters for military purposes hostile to the Union, and a resolution freeing federal officers from enforcing fugitive slave laws. In April 1862, a law was passed to emancipate immediately all slaves in the District of Columbia, with compensation of $300 per head to the slave-holders. On June 19, slavery was abolished without

Above: An African-American regiment being reviewed.

Right: Passing of the Thirteenth Amendment enacting the abolition of slavery, 1865.

Below: Confederate Robert E. Lee surrenders to General Ulysses Simpson Grant at the Appomatox Court House at the end of the American Civil War. Grant went on to become the eighteenth President of the United States.

compensation in all federal territories. On September 22, the Preliminary Emancipation Proclamation gave the rebel states 100 days in which to submit, or the irrevocable emancipation of their slaves would be announced.

Finally the Civil War was officially transformed into a war that would end slavery with the issue by President Lincoln on January 1, 1863 of the Emancipation Proclamation. This historic document declared that all those held as slaves in any state or part of a state in rebellion against the Union would be forever free. Although this was not the *de facto* abolition of slavery since by definition it covered only those areas outside Union control and did not apply either to conquered areas or to the slave holding states who had remained in the Union, it was of immense symbolic importance. Whatever the legal niceties, the remaining slaves throughout the South now knew that a Union victory would bring the ending of slavery. On the eve of that Union victory two years later Congress on January 31, 1865, passed by a two-thirds majority the Thirteenth Amendment to the United States Constitution which proclaimed that:

"Neither slavery nor involuntary servitude, except as a punishment for crime whereof the party shall have been duly convicted, shall exist within the United States, or any place subject to their jurisdiction."

Right and Below: A celebration of the abolition of slavery in Washington D.C.

7 Ending the Evil: the Aftermath of Abolition and Slavery in the Twentieth century

Despite the great and remarkable victories achieved by the abolitionist campaigns of the eighteenth and nineteenth centuries, the results of their efforts were not to prove the great new dawn of equal opportunity for all which the more radical protesters had anticipated. The passage of the Thirteenth Amendment to the United States Constitution on January 31, 1865, ended slavery on the North American mainland, but for the majority of newly liberated African-American people, it opened a difficult new chapter in which great hopes rapidly gave way to widespread disappointment. For the abolitionists, several more decades of campaigning, diplomatic, and military pressure were necessary to close off the last routes used for the export of slaves from Africa. In Africa itself, only the new forms of labor organization forcibly imposed in the aftermath of colonial partition brought a gradual end to the institutions of domestic slavery. Although mass slavery was then effectively eradicated by the 1940s, at the end of the twentieth century there remain sufficient instances of slavery and slave-like practices world-wide to require the attentions of a United Nations commission and the campaign against these last vestiges of an ancient evil goes on.

African-Americans: From Reconstruction to Civil Rights

In the months immediately after the conclusion of the Civil War the legislatures of the defeated Confederate states dismayed the newly liberated blacks and Northern public opinion by repeated efforts to pass so-called "black codes" that relegated their African-American populations to a status less than free by imposing restrictions on their

rights of property ownership and judicial access, as well as allowing the re-imposition of forced labor on those adjudged to be "vagrants." Although in the short term these moves were counterproductive, provoking Federal Reconstruction legislation that was more liberal than it might have otherwise been, they were also a grim reminder that racist opinions could not be so easily reconstructed and proved a precursor to more long-lasting "Jim Crow" laws once the reconstruction administrations had passed.

Awareness of the extent of continuing Southern resistance to fair treatment of African-American people prompted the Republican-controlled Congress to pass a series of measures including the 1866 Civil Rights Act, the 1867 Reconstruction Act, and the Fourteenth and Fifteenth Amendments. These required the Southern states to grant all citizens equal rights to property ownership and access to the law, and to extend the vote to all adult males, imposing a temporary administration on those states who had yet to comply and seek re-admission to Congress. Although the fact that the slave-holders had rebelled against the Union reduced their political influence in the short term and meant that, unlike in the Caribbean, they

Above right: In the Reconstruction era freed blacks rushed to take advantage of opportunities for education.

Below right: One of the Freedmen's Schools built in the South in the Reconstruction era.

Above: A post-war jury of whites and blacks. After the initial euphoria, white racism limited the hoped for integration throughout the South.

could be denied any compensation for the loss of their "property," pro-slavery apologists remained the dominant political force throughout the South. Even in the North there was little support for any positive measures to aid the newly-liberated blacks and the general feeling that they should be left to provide for themselves ignored the overwhelming hostility of Southern white interests. As a consequence the few measures that were taken to assist the ex-slaves were limited by half-hearted application and a general lack of adequate funding. The Freedmen's Bureau was established as a War Department agency in May 1865. Between then and 1868 it helped supervize the difficult transition to free labor in Southern agriculture and provided modest funding for black schools. Its intervention was bitterly criticized by many planters and Southern politicians, while some blacks felt its agents were liable to compromise their interests in a futile attempt to calm this opposition.

The calls by a small number of radical Congressmen for large-scale land redistribution programs to break up the plantations and resettle the freedmen on sustainable farms were easily defeated and the limited federal efforts to sponsor land reform were largely ineffective. President Johnson insisted on the reversal of the efforts by General W. T. Sherman in 1865 to redistribute land in the Sea Islands,

areas of South Carolina, and Georgia, and the Southern Homestead Act, which allowed the use of public land in five states, was handicapped by high costs and bureaucratic procedures.

The freed people themselves adapted as far as possible to the difficult conditions in which they found themselves, seeking out new ways of working wherever possible and resisting all attempts to constrain them into working practices such as labor gangs, which were reminiscent of slavery. Where there was no alternative to contracting as a plantation laborer, most at least sought not to work for their former master. Since direct land ownership was beyond the reach of the majority throughout most of the South they favored methods of working such as land rental and sharecropping, which gave a crucial degree of autonomy over matters such as working hours and conditions. There was also a gradual increase in black land-owning over the following decades.

Education was a major priority for freed people

Right: Former slave family settling in Nebraska after the Civil War.

Far right: Radical members of the First Legislature after the war.

Below: Office of the Freedmen's Bureau, which provided limited assistance to some ex-slaves after the Civil War.

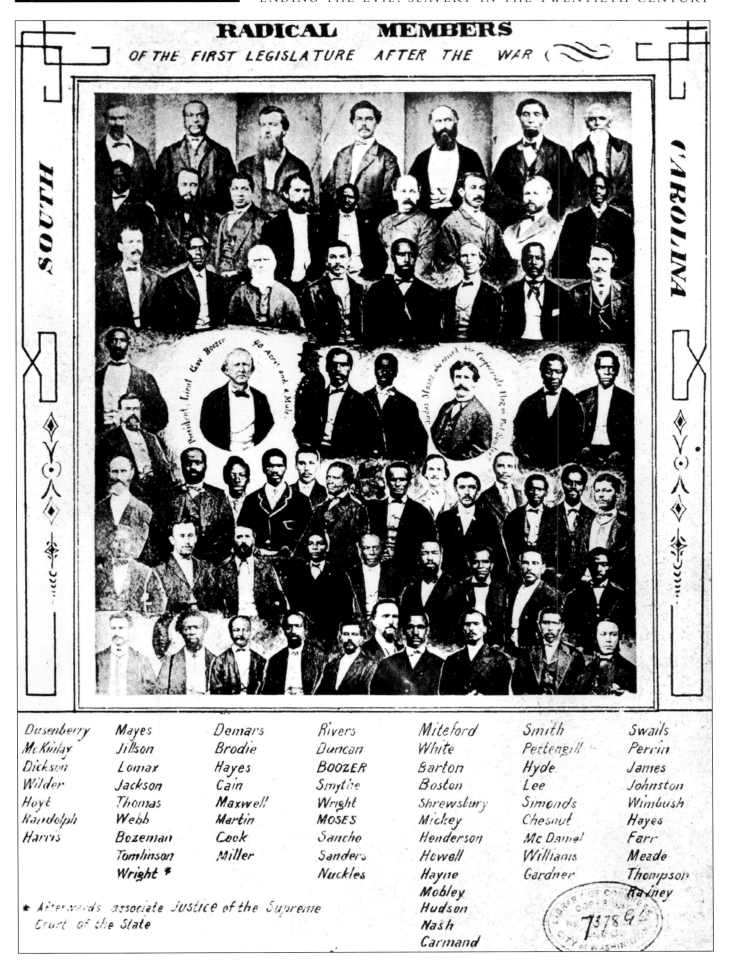

RADICAL MEMBERS
OF THE FIRST LEGISLATURE AFTER THE WAR

SOUTH CAROLINA

Dusenberry	Mayes	Demars	Rivers	Miteford	Smith	Swails
McKinlay	Jillson	Brodie	Duncan	White	Pettengill	Perrin
Dickson	Lomax	Hayes	BOOZER	Barton	Hyde	James
Wilder	Jackson	Cain	Smythe	Boston	Lee	Johnston
Hoyt	Thomas	Maxwell	Wright	Shrewsbury	Simonds	Wimbush
Randolph	Webb	Martin	MOSES	Mickey	Chesnut	Hayes
Harris	Bozeman	Cook	Sancho	Henderson	Mc Daniel	Farr
	Tomlinson	Miller	Sanders	Howell	Williams	Meade
	Wright *		Nuckles	Hayne	Gardner	Thompson
				Mobley		Rainey
				Hudson		
				Nash		
				Carmand		

* Afterwards associate Justice of the Supreme Court of the State

Far left, top: "Slavery is Dead?" A poster protesting at continued exploitation of blacks in the aftermath of emancipation.

Far left, bottom: "The Shackle Broken—by the Genius of Freedom."

Above: The first colored senator and representatives in Congress.

Left: An African-American family in Kentucky after the war.

CELEBRATION AT BALTIMORE ON MAY 19th 1870.

Left: Two members of the Klu Klux Klan in their disguises.

Above: A contemporary print illustrating the aftermath of the passage of the Fifteenth Amendment.

throughout the South. The schools set up by the Freedmen's Bureau and Northern-sponsored benevolent societies were massively over-subscribed as both adults and children flooded to take advantage of the new opportunities despite the often high fees. The reconstruction governments could provide only limited funds for these schools and considerable local input was required in such basics as the construction of school buildings and furniture. Black churches also played an important role in the community life of the South. For the brief period of the reconstruction, African-American politicians were elected in quite substantial numbers to serve at local, state, and even federal levels.

In the 1870s, however, the failure of the reconstruction administrations to satisfy the often unrealistic expectations of their supporters and to appease their opponents had led to widespread disillusionment with the entire direction of Southern politics. One by one the state governments were overthrown and replaced by conservative Democratic administrations. The stage was set for decades that would be marked by increased anti-black violence, ever-growing restrictions on black civil rights, enforced segregation, and unequal facilities, and in consequence the beginning of a massive migration to the industrial cities of the North. Almost a century was to pass before the development of the Civil Rights Movement in the 1950s and 1960s began the still continuing struggle to roll back this legacy and demand an equal status for African-Americans in the United States.

Africa and the End of the Export Trade

Although Brazil did not finally abolish slavery until 1888, the combined effects of the closure of markets in the Americas, the naval blockade, and of increasing British intervention on the African mainland, effectively ended the transatlantic shipment of slaves by the end of the 1860s. At this time however quite large numbers of slaves were

The Arabian Connection

The famous explorer and missionary David Livingstone helped draw attention to the evils of Arab slave trading in East Africa in the 1870s:

"In less time than I take to talk about it, these unfortunate creatures—84 of them, wended their way into the village where we were. Some of them, the eldest, were women from 20 to 22 years of age, and there were youths from 18 to 19, but the large majority was made up of boys and girls from 7 years to 14 or 15 years of age. A more terrible scene than these men, women and children, I do not think I ever came across. To say that they were emaciated would not give you an idea of what human beings can undergo under certain circumstances . . . Each of them had his neck in a large forked stick, weighing from 30 to 40 pounds, and five or six feet long, cut with a fork at the end of it where the branches of a tree spread out . . . The women were tethered with bark thongs, which are, of all things, the most cruel to be tied with. Of course they are soft and supple when first striped off the trees, but a few hours in the sun make them about as hard as the iron round packing-cases. The little children were fastened by thongs to their mothers. (The travellers released the slaves.) As we passed along the path which these slaves had travelled . . . I was shown a spot in the bushes where a poor woman the day before, unable to keep on the march, and likely to hinder it, was cut down by the axe of one of these slave drivers . . . We went on further and were shown a place where a child lay. It had been recently born, and its mother was unable to carry it from debility and exhaustion; so the slave-trader had taken this little infant by its feet and dashed its brains out against one of the trees and thrown it in there."

Right: David Livingstone (1813–1873), the missionary, traveler, and explorer, preaches to native villagers. The churches established by Livingstone and other missionaries were able to provide refuge for fugitive slaves throughout much of East Africa, hastening the collapse of domestic slavery. *The Graphic - published 1887*

Far right: Three captured African slave traders, apprehended in 1892 during British attempts to suppress the continuing slave trade in East Africa and the Indian Ocean.

still being exported by the three remaining routes, across the Sahara, the Red Sea, and the Indian Ocean. British diplomatic pressure on the Ottoman States of North Africa and the Middle East, and on Ethiopia, had resulted in the passage of official measures abolishing slave trading in both areas in the 1850s, but no efforts at enforcement had been undertaken and they remained completely ineffectual. The expansion of Egyptian rule into Sudan and the Red Sea under the leadership of Muhammed Ali from the 1820s had actually increased the trans-Saharan trade as some 10,000 men a year were sent to Egypt to be forcibly recruited into the Egyptian army. Red Sea ports such as Massawa were used to ship some 6,000 slaves a year captured in southern Ethiopia to Egypt and Arabia. Most of these were children, with young women under twenty in particular demand. Only the direct intervention of the British in Egypt and, paradoxically, the defeat of both British and Egyptian interests in Sudan by the Islamic jihad of Muhammed Ahmed (the Mahdi), in the 1880s, brought about a marked decline in these figures. In East Africa slaves were captured for export to Arabia and India, for use in the plantation economies of the Indian Ocean, and until around 1850 for the transatlantic trade. Under the control of Omani Arabs and local Swahili traders, plantation economies, producing mostly cloves for export to India, employed large numbers of slaves. A treaty outlawing exports to the North signed by the Omani regime in Zanzibar in 1822 was not enforced. Arab slavers in East Africa became the focus of abolitionist propaganda and related missionary efforts, initiated by David Livingstone, throughout the second half of the nineteenth century. It was only the establishment of colonial rule and the partition of East Africa between the British, French, German, Belgian, and Portuguese that brought a gradual end to the export of slaves from the regime. In Zanzibar, the African population waited until after the end of British rule to exact a bloody revenge on their Arab oppressors, killing a significant proportion of them in a single night of revolution in 1964.

Throughout Africa the ending of the export trade had the paradoxical effect of increasing the use of slaves in local agriculture and promoting the spread of a "slave mode of production." The mechanisms that had evolved for the

Above: The Nuba of Central Sudan have been raided for slaves by their Arab neighbors for many centuries. Today they are still suffering from attacks by the Islamic regime, with widespread rumors that captured women are forced to work as slaves.

Right: African-American cow punchers in Bonham, Texas. African-Americans filled a huge range of roles in many of the most difficult and inhospitable regions of the Americas.

capture, transport, and marketing of huge numbers of slaves each year to supply the export markets were still in place, but the cutting off of the huge overseas demand led inevitably to a fall in slave prices. This made them more accessible to local slave owners. At the same time the shift in European mercantile interest towards so-called "legitimate trade" increased the demand for the products of African agriculture and therefore the incentive to mobilize labor through slavery in their production. Palm oil was perhaps the most important commodity in this growing export trade, although it was atypical in being produced largely on small holdings rather than the large-scale plantations on which cotton and other crops were generally grown. Large numbers of Africans continued to be incorporated in these systems of slavery throughout the final decades of the nineteenth century.

Although the supposed abolition of this type of slavery

had provided one of the main justifications for the European partition and colonization of Africa following the Berlin Conference of 1884–85, the new colonial regimes were in practice extremely reluctant to move against local slave-holding. In some cases, as with the purchase of slaves to be incorporated in the French army in Senegal, and the distribution among the soldiers of women captured on expeditions as late as 1891, the local administrations were themselves involved in slave trading. More generally they were aware of the importance of slave workers to the agricultural output of their colonies and anxious to avoid any measures that would offend the local rulers on whose collaboration they often relied.

However, both the intervention of abolitionist-inclined missionaries and the actions of the enslaved peoples themselves forced the British and French regimes in particular to move to abolish slave-holding more quickly than they desired. Many missionaries provided places of refuge for fugitive slaves who often provided the majority of their early converts. Since the authorities could not risk outraging domestic sentiment by preventing missionary activity, and many officials were themselves reluctant to actually go as far as returning fugitives to their masters, domestic slavery declined rapidly in the face of large-scale desertions from plantations wherever colonial rule was established. In Ghana whole villages of slaves were deserting en masse by the 1880s, while in French West Africa the system of slave production effectively collapsed with the flight of hundreds of thousands in the 1904–1906.

New systems of organizing labor were imposed in the African colonies. While for many this involved a participation for the first time in wage labor, necessitated by the requirement for money to pay newly imposed taxes, forced and unpaid labor was also used for many projects including road building. The continued activities of abolitionists were directed in particular to preventing the most outrageous excesses, of which the brutal regime imposed by King Leopold of Belgium in his vast personal domain of the Congo was the most terrible example.

A report by the Irish patriot Sir Roger Casement, commissioned by the British Government drew world attention to the systematic infliction of punishments ranging from whipping, through mutilation, to execution imposed by Leopold's agents on people who failed to gather their quota of rubber. The king became an international pariah before finally agreeing to allow the annexation of the ironically-named Congo Free State by Belgium in 1908.

Left: Irish patriot and British consular official Sir Roger David Casement (1864-1916) wrote the report which drew world-wide attention to the atrocities being committed in the so-called Congo Free State by agents of King Leopold of Belgium.

One of the most far-reaching effects of slavery has been the establishment of a diaspora of Africans throughout much of the world, most obviously in the Americas, but also in Europe, the Middle East, and India. Although the extent of contacts between these peoples and their ancestral homelands varies, Africa remains for many an important cornerstone for a sense of cultural identity that has found expression in movements as varied as Rastafarianism and Afrocentricity.

While many scholars regard the return of Africans to Liberia under the auspices of white-sponsored African colonization projects to have been ill-conceived, the mid-nineteenth century provides a rare example of a limited number of Africans who were actually able to return home voluntarily and rebuild a life in the country of their mothers, making an important contribution to the development of Nigeria.

From about 1850 two groups of ex-slaves began to return in quite substantial numbers mostly to the Yoruba-speaking region of South-western Nigeria. The largest number came from the community established at Freetown, Sierra Leone, populated by those rescued by the British Navy in the cause of their anti-slavery blockade. In Sierra Leone they had adopted a Europeanized Creole lifestyle as a result of missionary education. Many of those who chose to return to Nigeria on chartered ships in the 1860s and 1970s played a prominent role in the spread of Christianity among the Yoruba, and later they were important figures in the development of Nigerian nationalist politics.

In the 1890s there was a movement both in Lagos and in Freetown, to abandon European names and dress styles in favor of local forms. Joining these returnees in Lagos was a second, less influential group of several thousand ex-slaves who purchased their freedom in Brazil and returned via the shipping route linking Lagos and Bahia. Amongst the legacies of these "Brazilians" was a fashion for Luso-Brazilian architectural styles among the wealthy in Nigeria that lasted into the 1950s.

Slavery in the Twentieth Century

In 1962 Saudi Arabia became the last country in the world to pass a law abolishing the legal status of slavery. Article Four of the 1948 Universal Declaration of Human Rights states that, "No one shall be held in slavery and servitude. Slavery and the slave trade shall be prohibited in all their forms." Yet as the twentieth century draws to a close it is clear that slavery and similar practices of enforced labor are by no means confined to the past. The United Nations Economic and Social Council maintains a "Working Group on Contemporary Forms of Slavery" that publishes regular reports on occurrences of slavery in many parts of the world today. Abolitionist organizations such as "Anti-Slavery International" in Britain and others around the world continue to campaign to bring a final end to slavery. Early in 1998 four anti-slavery activists from a group called "SOS-Esclaves" were jailed in Mauritania in north-west Africa after they gave an interview to French television about the continued existence of slavery in their country. A number of reports on the situation in Mauritania published by the U.N. working party make it clear that, despite official denials, large numbers of people descended from sub-Saharan Africans brought into the country by the slave trade in past generations are still kept forcibly in a servile state by the ruling class of Moors. Elsewhere in Africa there is concern over the enslavement of Dinka women and children for use as farm laborers and domestic servants in the long running civil war in Sudan.

Although some of the forms of forced labor with which anti-slavery campaigners are involved today, such as the widespread exploitation of child labor, differ substantially from the chattel slavery we have been exploring in this book, others such as the continued use of bonded labor and the trafficking in women and children for the purposes of prostitution are clearly contemporary modifications of an age old problem. Bonded labor involves the pledging of labor for a long period of time in a usually fruitless effort to pay of a debt. Often, "wages" are set at extremely low levels and spurious charges made for rent and food keep a worker and his family in permanent bondage. Such systems are widespread in parts of Asia and Latin America, and are particularly prevalent in the exploitation of Native Americans in Brazil. The use of force to procure women and children for prostitution often involves large payments being made to purchase the victims, either from their families or gangs of organized criminals. The practice has been documented in countries such as India, Thailand, and the Philippines, and in the supply of women from both south-east Asia and Eastern Europe to the sex industry in parts of Western Europe.

Although changing intellectual climates, the activities of Abolitionists, and the resistance of enslaved peoples themselves have transformed labor relations around the world, and slavery no longer plays the central role it has at many times in the past, it remains a sad fact that is still a very real prospect for hundreds of thousands of people on the eve of the twenty-first century.

Below: A U.S. army truck loaded with liberated Russian, Polish and Ukrainian slave laborers in a German town.

Right: A Haitian man about to begin a voodoo ceremony in the village of Marbial.

Right: Soldiers in the street during race riots in America hide their faces from the camera, 1961.

Overleaf: Dr. Martin Luther King, American clergyman and civil rights campaigner who promoted a non-violent struggle for equality, March 1965.

Appendices

1 Chronology

Mesopotamia c. 3500 B.C.–c. 500B.C.

The civilizations developed from ancient Sumer were based on elaborate city states built and maintained by slave labor. Most slaves worked as laborers or fulfilled other duties for one of the two dominant social institutions of these communities: the royal palace or the temple. Slaves were shaved and shackled in chains, and frequently branded with the sign of their owner. There is some evidence that locally-born slaves were obliged to work for only a limited period, in some cases three years, before their debt was discharged and they were set free.

Sources of slaves: Men and women captured in the course of warfare, and citizens who might fall socially into the status of slaves as a result of unpaid debt.

Egypt c. 2200 B.C.–c. 200 A.D.

Scholars have often noted that slavery was a marginal institution in ancient Egypt and did not really become widespread until the Late Period (after c. 700 B.C.). Slavery as a recognized legal status, in which an individual could be bought and sold, can be seen from a number of surviving documents recording contracts of sale. These slaves were legally prohibited from owning any property themselves. The limited evidence suggests that the majority of slaves were well treated within a paternalistic relationship with their masters, and there are isolated reports of slaves rising to become high-rank officials.

Sources of slaves: Mostly foreigners captured in warfare or purchased from abroad, although there is some evidence that native Egyptians were themselves obliged, perhaps as a penalty for crime or because of absolute poverty, to become slaves.

Greece 750 B.C.–146 B.C.

In contrast to the limited use of slaves in Egypt, the civilization that developed in Greece can be classified as a slave society. In other words, Greece had a society in which the institution of slavery was a fundamental aspect of social organization. Slavery in ancient Greece was not regarded as an unfortunate but necessary evil; instead it was at the core of the political organization and self-conception of the Greek city states.

Sources of slaves: Prisoners of war were a legitimate source of slaves, and both Greeks and non-Greeks in the Mediterranean also lost their freedom by falling into the hands of pirates. Other important sources of slaves included the natural reproduction of the existing slave population, purchase from trade with non-Greek sources, the disposal of unwanted babies, and the enslavement of insolvent debtors. Large-scale slave markets became established at Chios, Samos, Ephesus, Cyprus, and Athens.

Rome 753 B.C–746 A.D.

The Romans took the institution onto a dramatic new scale. It has been suggested that a conservative estimate would put the number of slaves in Italy when Augustus became emperor in 31 B.C., at the conclusion of the Republican era, at around two million.

Sources of slaves: The primary source was the capture of huge numbers of men, women, and children in the course of warfare. During his conquest of Gaul, Julius Caesar took some one million prisoners, while in 167 B.C., 150,000 captive Epirotes were brought back to Rome for sale after a single battle. Kidnapping and piracy were also a constant threat. The natural reproduction of the existing slave population was also an important source, with any children born to slave mothers becoming slaves themselves, regardless of the status of the father. Additionally, many poor people, unable to sustain themselves as tenant farmers, or facing famine beyond the Empire's borders, would voluntarily offer themselves and their families for sale as slaves, knowing that they would be guaranteed a minimal sustenance. Finally there was the widely practiced custom known as "exposing," where unwanted babies were simply left outside. Although there are records of some sub-Saharan African slaves, and African people were enslaved in the Roman provinces of Egypt and North Africa, there is no evidence that slaves were a significant component of the trade that already criss-crossed the Sahara.

404 B.C.

It is reported that the Roman noblewoman Messalina freed 8,000 slaves after she espoused Christianity.

135 B.C.

6,000 slaves of Syrian origin rebel in Sicily. Conflict continues over several years before order is restored.

104 B.C.

Second large uprising in Sicily takes several years and an invading army of 17,000 Roman legionnaires to supress a slave force said to number 30,000.

73 B.C.

Spartacus, a Thracian who escaped with a small group of followers from a gladiatorial training school at Capua, rapidly established a growing band of Thracian, Celtic, and German slaves who plundered and devastated a large area of Italy.

71 B.C.

Spartacus was killed in battle in 71 B.C. and 6,000 of his captured followers were executed by crucifixion along the Appian Way.

595 A.D.

Pope Gregory the Great sends a priest called Candidus to Britain to buy pagan slave boys to work on monastic estates.

732 A.D.

Battle of Poitiers. From this date until around 1000 A.D. slavs from Bosnia become the major source of slaves for Islamic society.

Below: "*Non Angli, sed Angeli.*" Saint Gregory and the British slaves. (From an egraving by J.C. Armytage after a painting by Keeley Halswelle.)

1324

Mansa Mura makes his pilgrimage to Mecca. Accompanying him are 500 slaves each carrying a gold staff. This heralds a new more intensive phase of sub–Saharan African slave trading.

1402–05

Soon after the Canary Islands are discovered by the Portuguese, colonization begins using the forced labor of African slaves.

1418

Portuguese sailors begin to sail down the unexplored coast of west Africa.

1434

Portuguese captain Gil Eannes successfully returns from a voyage beyond Cape Bojador, breaching a previously much feared frontier of the known world.

1447

The Danish captain and most of the crew of a Portuguese vessel are killed by local people in a naval battle off the island of Gorée. After these early setbacks the practice of negotiating with local African rulers and winning their consent to engage in trade of both slaves and goods becomes the norm throughout the history of the Atlantic trade.

1463

Bosnian trade ended after conquest by Ottoman Turks.

1470

The gold producing regions of the Gold Coast are reached.

1480

Diego Cão, on a voyage sponsored by the crown, makes contact with the kingdom of Kongo.

1485–86

Regular trade begins with the kingdom of Benin.

1488

Bartolomeu Dias reaches the southern tip of Africa, opening up Portuguese trade into the Indian Ocean.

1492

Columbus discovers the New World.

1494

The Spanish are prevented by the Treaty of Tordesillas, signed after Papal mediation, from establishing colonies in Africa. This leaves the Portuguese with a monopoly of the transatlantic trade until the closing years of the sixteenth century.

1510

King Ferdinand of Spain authorizes the purchase of 250 Africans in Lisbon to be carried to his territories in New Spain. This signals the beginning of the Atlantic trade.

1562–69

John Hawkins, an English naval commander of the Elizabethan period, leads three expeditions to Africa during which slaves are taken for sale to the Spanish colonies in the West Indies.

1568–1648

The Eighty Years War. The Dutch assault on the maritime empire of the Portuguese and Spanish. By the 1630s and 1640s Dutch naval superiority allows them to take both the Pernambuco sugar-plantation region of Brazil and important African slave supplying areas, including Gorée, the fort of El Mina in the Gold Coast, and coastal regions of Angola, from the Portuguese.

1605–06

The maroon mini-state of Palmares is established in the Brazilian rain forest.

1619

Slaves beginning to be imported into the North American colonies, originally by a few Dutch settlers in Virginia.

1670

The growth of the tobacco industry in North America precipitates a concurrent growth in the the slave population.

1672

The Royal Africa Society is chartered in Britain, and establishes a string of forts on the African coast. Between 1673 and 1689 it is responsible for the export of some 89,000 slaves after which its monopoly is broken by independant traders.

1680

Virginia's first major slave code restricts the rights of blacks, both free and slaves, in Northern and Southern colonies.

1688

Quakers in Pennsylvania print "The Germantown Protest," expressing anti-slavery sentiments.

Right: "Remarkably as though it were a dance." An artist of the 1790s depicts the landing in North America of a group of Africans to be sold as slaves.

1695

November: Palmares overrun by Portuguese troops.

1730

Britain becomes the dominant slave trading nation. Between 1690 and 1807 in the region of 2.8 million slaves are transported by the British.

1734

William Snelgrove publishes book of slave mutinies on board ship.

1737

700 slaves die in the wreck of Dutch ship *Leusden*.

1760

America begins direct participation in the transatlantic slave trade. American slave traders carry some 425,000 Africans, a large proportion of whom were landed in Brazil and Cuba.

"Tacky's Rebellion" takes place—the most bloody of the numerous revolts in the British colonies of the Caribbean.

1772

British Lord Justice Lord Mansfield rules that there is no positive support for slavery in English law.

1775–83

The American Revolution. One of the most marked effects of the Revolutionary era was to translate the economic divide that had long existed between the slave-based societies of the South and the states of the North, where slavery was economically marginal, into a growing sense of a moral and social divide based on attitudes towards slavery.

1775

November: The Governor of Virginia promises freedom to slaves who take up arms against the British.

1776

Adam Smith's influential book, *The Wealth of Nations*, is published. This work was a vicious attack on the mercantile system that benefited from slavery.

1781

November 29: The *Zong* Atrocity. 232 slaves are thrown overboard in order that the ship's owners may claim compensation from the insurance company.

1783

The *Zong* Atrocity. English courts uphold the claim for reimbursement. This results in widespread outrage and an upsurge in abolitionism.

A witness who sailed on the *Brookes* records that they packed in over 600 slaves on the 320-ton ship, with over 70 dying on the crossing.

1787

The passage of laws barring the extension of slavery in newly colonized areas, such as the act of 1787 covering the present states of Ohio, Michigan, Indiana, Illinois, and Wisconsin. Both Congress and a number of states moved to prohibit the import of new slaves, although Congress was prevented by a compromise agreement at the Constitutional Convention of 1787 from introducing such a ban until 1807.

William Wilberforce becomes spokesman and leader of British abolitionists.

Josiah Wedgwood, the leading pioneer of the industrial production of pottery, founds the "Society for the Abolition of the Slave Trade." Wedgwood designs and widely distributes some 200,000 copies of a pottery seal for the society, whose motif was a kneeling African in chains, with the words "Am I not a man and a brother?" around the edge.

1788

Wilberforce's influence with leading political figures leads the Prime Minister to appoint a Committee of the Privy Council to investigate the slave trade.

English abolitionists first publish the notorious print of slaves packed together on the Liverpool ship *Brookes.*

1789

The French Revolution. The unstable political climate that follows the revolution allows an attempted uprising in French Haiti in 1790.

1791

August: With local politics in turmoil, a new slave revolt erupts in Haiti. By late September over a thousand plantations have been burned and hundreds of whites killed, with many more blacks murdered in reprisals.

1792–1802

French revolutionary wars in Europe.

1792

The arrival of 6,000 French troops in Haiti briefly stabilizes the situation, although significant areas remain in rebel hands.

1793

The Fugitive Slave Law, allows slave-holders to regain possession of any fugitives.

The development of the cotton gin prompts a rapid expansion of cotton growing across the Southern states

Left: William Pitt the Younger (1759–1806) from an engraving by F. Bartolozzi c. 1790.

and finances the opening up of huge new areas to agriculture.

Haiti. The outbreak of war with Spain and England led both the Republican administration and the Spanish to arm black rebels as mercenaries. Facing an English invasion the desperate regime declared all slavery abolished on August 29, 1793.

1798
British finally evacuate the remnants of their invasion force from Haiti, having lost 15,000 out of 25,000 men to a combination of rampant diseases and combat deaths.

1799
Thirty-nine slaves go blind on board French ship *Le Rodeur*. They are thrown into the sea.

1800
Gabriel Prosser leads a slave rebellion in Virginia.

1803
A French re-invasion force of some 44,000 troops sent by

Napoleon to restore slavery in Haiti is defeated, although it does succeed in kidnapping slave leader Toussaint l'Ouverture, who dies in a French dungeon on April 7.

1806
A coalition government led by the pro-abolitionists Grenville and Fox is formed in Britain.

A partial Abolition Bill is finally passed in Britain, prohibiting the sale of slaves to foreign lands or their importation into the newly gained colonies in the Caribbean.

1807
The passage of a more sweeping measure under which, from January 1, 1808, "all manner of dealing and trading in slaves" is "utterly abolished, prohibited and declared to be unlawful" throughout the British Empire.

1811
In Britain slave trading becomes a crime punishable by transportation or death.

1816
British attempts to draft an international treaty setting up a permanent bureau to effect abolition fail in the face of French and Russian opposition.

1817
The Spanish sign a treaty under which they receive £400,000 compensation from the British in return for an agreement to outlaw trading.

1819
Congress debates the admission of Missouri to the Union. Missouri's state constitution not only provides for slavery but also bars any immigration into Missouri of free blacks from other states. As abolitionists point out, this violates the article of the Constitution granting equal privileges and immunities to all citizens. Eventually, the so-called Missouri Compromise is reached, under which the state is admitted along with its existing pro-slavery laws but slavery becomes prohibited in further areas of the Louisiana Purchase territories north of latitude 36' 30".

1822
A treaty is signed outlawing exports to the North by the Omani regime in Zanzibar, although this is not enforced.

Left: A liberated slave.

Above left: Ben Franklin's reception by the French court.

Arab slavers in East Africa became the focus of abolitionist propaganda and related missionary efforts initiated by David Livingstone.

Slave rebellion in South Carolina led by Denmark Vassey.

1823
British government passed laws to reform existing slave conditions throughout the British West Indies. Among these was the abolition of the whip and of flogging female slaves, as well as the freeing of all female children born after 1823.

Forty-seven slaves hanged after a rebellion in Demerara.

1831
Slave uprising in Virginia is led by Nat Turner.

France finally signs the first of a series of treaties but continued opposition to British intervention with the free passage of French ships largely overrides the growing pro-abolitionist sentiment in the country.

The Liberator, edited by William Lloyd Garrison is published in Boston and continues until 1865, it is perhaps the most influential and effective of the regular newspapers.

1832
100 slaves executed in Jamaica following an uprising.

1833
The Duke of Wellington opposes the Abolition Bill in British Parliament.

The American Anti-Slavery Society is founded, bringing together abolitionists from New England, where William Lloyd Garrison was the most prominent activist, with those from Philadelphia, and from the newly opened up states of the Midwest.

August 29: The Bill for the Abolition of Slavery becomes law in Britain. The continued influence of the planters is, however, marked by the granting of £20 million in compensation for the loss of their "property" and the requirement that the freedmen be obliged to serve a further seven years as apprentices.

1840
Thomas Clarkson addresses an anti-slavery convention at Freemason Hall, London.

1841
The Great Anti-Slavery Meeting takes place at Exeter Hall, London.

1844
A revolt on board an American ship the *Kentucky*, during which forty-six men and one woman are punished horrifically by being hanged, mutilated while still alive, shot, and thrown into the sea.

1845

Frederick Douglass publishes his autobiography, *Narrative of the Life of Frederick Douglass, an American Slave*. This volume proves to be hugely influential.

1846–48

Mexican–American War. The Union acquires vast new territories and heated debate breaks out over Mexico's existing slave laws.

1847

Zamba, son of a slave trading African chief, publishes an account of his life as a slave.

1849

Harriet Tubman reaches the North. Following her escape she makes a total of nineteen journeys from her home in Auburn, New York, to lead others, including her own parents, to freedom on the "Underground Railroad."

1850

August–September: Congress passes a series of five measures, negotiated by Senator Henry Clay of Kentucky, which become known as the Compromise of 1850. The slave trade is abolished in the District of Columbia and the admission of California as a free state is approved. New Mexico and Utah are opened to settlement by both slaveholders and non-slavers, while Texas, already admitted as a slave state, is compensated for giving up claims to adjoining territory. Most controversially, the new and strengthened Fugitive Slave Act is passed.

1851

Harriet Beecher Stowe's *Uncle Tom's Cabin* first published in serial form.

1854

A Boston crowd attempts to rescue escapee Antony Burns from government forces.

The Kansas-Nebraska Act allows settlers to formulate their own position on slavery thus breaching the 1820 Accords for the prohibition of slavery north of 36' 30".

1856

May 24: In a fight at Pottawatomie Creek, John Brown and his sons avenge the murders of several abolitionists by killing five terrorists.

1857

A ruling finally emerges from the Supreme Court in the long-running Dred Scott case. It argues that the Missouri

Right: Refugee slaves were also in danger of capture by free blacks desperate to earn money.

Compromise is unconstitutional since Congress lacks the power to prohibit slavery in any part of the Union.

Above: The Harper's Ferry Insurrection, during which John Brown was wounded.

1859

October 16: John Brown seizes control of the armory at Harper's Ferry. Ten of Brown's men, including two of his sons, are killed in the fighting that follows, and the wounded Brown is captured and charged with crimes including treason and murder. He is hanged forty days later. Despite the dismal failure of his attack, the impact on the abolition movement and the climate of opinion in both the North and the South is electric.

1860

Presidential election is won by Abraham Lincoln, on a platform which includes limited opposition to slavery.

1861–65

The American Civil War. The split between the slave-holding Southern states and the increasingly hostile North widens over the course of the early decades of the nineteenth century, as disputes arise over the admission of new states to the Union and over slave-holders, attempts to recapture fugitives. The emergence of an organized abolition movement in the North, uniting both blacks and whites in an often bitter struggle, is to be a key factor in keeping the issue at the forefront of public attention and mobilizing support to push for new measures in Congress. Pro-slavery apologists in the South become increasingly extreme as their national and international isolation increases. The attempts at political compromise, intended to hold the Union together in the face of these irreconcilable conflicts, finally collapse at the end of the 1850s with the attempted secession of the South. Although the resulting Civil War is fought primarily to restore the Union, it rapidly becomes apparent that victory for the Union forces will involve the ending of slavery.

1861

April 12: Southern attack on Fort Sumter in Charleston, South Carolina, heralds the attempted secession of the South and begins the civil war.

August: The Confiscation Act effectively frees any slaves used by their masters for military purposes hostile to the Union. A resolution is also passed which frees federal officers from enforcing fugitive slave laws.

1862

May: The first large scale recruitment of blacks to the Union army is made—without explicit authorization—by the pro-abolitionist General David Hunter. He begins to organize and train a regiment of some 800 black soldiers. However, the administration refuses to grant the necessary authorization and the general is forced to disband the regiment in August.

August: This decision is quickly reversed and Brigadier General Rufus is given permission to recruit up to 5,000 black slodiers.

April: A law is passed to emancipate immediately all slaves in the District of Columbia, with compensation of $300 per head to the slave-holders.

June 19: Slavery is abolished, without compensation, in all federal territories.

July: The second Confiscation Act makes it an offence for any member of the Union armed forces to give up fugitive slaves.

September 22: The Preliminary Emancipation Proclamation gives the rebel states 100 days in which to submit, or face the irrevocable emancipation of their slaves.

1863

January 1: The Civil War is officially transformed into a war that will end slavery with the issue, by President Lincoln, of the Emancipation Proclamation. This historic document declares that all those held as slaves in any state or part of a state in rebellion against the Union will be forever free.

1865

President Johnson insists on the reversal of efforts by General W. T. Sherman to redistribute land in the Sea Islands areas of South Carolina, and Georgia.

The Southern Homestead Act, which allows the use of public land in five states, confering title on it by a small payment and residence of five years, is handicapped by high costs and bureaucratic procedures.

January 31: Passed by a two-thirds majority, the Thirteenth Amendment to the United States Constitution proclaims freedom for all slaves throughout the United States.

May: The Freedmen's Bureau is established and helps to supervize the transition to free labor in Southern agriculture. It also provides some funding for black schools.

1866

Congress passed the Civil Rights Act.

1867

Congress passes the Reconstruction Act and the Fourteenth and Fifteenth Amendments.

1884

Following the Berlin Conference, Europe partitions and colonizes Africa primarily in an attempt to stop various

Phillis Wheatley

The eighteenth century slave Phillis Wheatley was to become one of America's best loved poets.

She was born on the western coast of Africa, probably in Senegal, in about 1753, and it was from here that she was kidnapped by slavers at about eight years of age and transported to America. Considered too young for the rigors of the sugar plantations of the West Indies or the cotton fields of the Southern colonies, she was taken to Boston and was consequently purchased by a tailor, John Wheatley, as a maid for his wife. Adhering to tradition, her original name, Fatou, was replaced with that of her master.

The Wheatleys were resolved to provide their young slave with a rudimentary education, and began to teach her to read and write. To their surprise, Phillis proved extrodinarily adept, and within sixteen months of her arrival in America she was proficient in English, Greek, and Latin, as well as history, geography and astronomy. Her first poem was published in the

Newport and Rhode Island Mercury on December 21, 1767.

In spite of this initial success, it proved impossible for Phillis to find a Boston publisher who would consider her work. Eventually, she and the Wheatley's were forced to look across the Atlantic, and after a trip to London, her first volume (the only one to be published within her lifetime) was produced in 1773. The collection, *Poems on Various Subjects, Religious and Moral*, contained thirty-nine original poems by Phillis and has a place in history as the first poetry published by an African-American.

Soon after their return from England the Wheatleys gave Phillis her freedom and she married a free black man, John Peters, though this union was dissolved after the irresponsible Peters abandoned her. To provide for herself, Phillis subsequently took a job as a servant and she died in poverty in 1784.

Although Phillis was a vociferous speaker against slavery, she was very much constrained by the poetical forms of the eighteenth century. Influenced by Pope, the most successful poet of the era, Phillis wrote Augustan Neo-Classical verse, within which there was no space for her private thoughts on the institution of slavery. In addition, her work was produced under strictly imposed ideological conditions; her natural genius was expected to maintain servility and gratitude to her superiors while refraining from any kind of political activism. The differences between her pastoral, rustic poetry and the righteous anger of her many letters and private notes is striking.

In this short verse, Wheatley makes her only poetic reference to her position as a slave. It is interesting that in the last verse she uses the word "refined." This can be read as illusion to the refining process that was applied, by her masters, to her own work; like the sugar refining process in the West Indies, turning black molasses into white sugar.

On Being Brought from Africa to America

'Twas mercy brought me from my pagan land,
Taught my benighted soul to understand
That there's a God, that there's a Saviour too:
Once I redemption neither sought nor knew.
Some view our race with scornful eye:
'Their colour is a diabolic dye.'
Remember Christians, negroes black as Cain
May be refined and join th' angelic train.

forms of slavery. However, the new colonial regimes prove unwilling to move against local slave-holding.

1888
Brazil finally abolishes slavery.

1904–06
In French West Africa the system of slave production effectively collapses with the flight of hundreds of thousands from local plantations.

1908
A report by the Irish patriot Sir Roger Casement, commissioned by the British Government, draws world attention to the systematic infliction of punishments ranging from whipping, through mutilation, to execution imposed by King Leopold of Belgium's agents on people who fail to gather their quota of rubber in his huge personal estates in the Congo. The king becomes an international pariah before finally agreeing to allow the annexation of the Congo Free State by Belgium

1944
Eric Williams, former chief minister of Trinidad and Tobago, publishes his respected work, *Capitalism and Slavery*.

1948
Universal Declaration of Human Rights

1955
Martin Luther King Jr. reaches prominence in the American civil rights movement.

1962
Saudi Arabia become the last country in the world to pass a law abolishing the legal status of slavery.

1964
In Zanzibar, the African population exacts a bloody revenge on its Arab oppressors, following the end of British rule, killing a significant proportion of them in a single night of revolution.

1968
April 4: Martin Luther King Jr. assassinated in Memphis, Tennessee.

1998
Four anti-slavery activists from a group called "SOS-Esclaves" are jailed in Mauritania in north-west Africa after giving an interview to French television about the continued existence of slavery in their country.

Far right: American writer Alex Haley, author of the book *Roots*, which did so much to raise awareness of the issues of slavery in the United States.

Right: Nation of Islam spokesperson Malcolm X (1925-1965) during a talk at Queens College, New York.

2 Statistics

Estimated slave imports 1526-1810

Area imported to	Number
Brazil	3,647,000
British Caribbean	1,665,000
British North America & US	399,000
Danish	28,000
Dutch America	500,000
Europe	175,000
French America	1,600,000
Spanish America	1,552,000

Estimated slave imports by 000s 1526-1810

Country imported to	Number
Argentina, Uruguay, Paraguay & Bolivia	100
Bahamas	10
Barbados	387
Bermuda	5
Brazil	3,647
British North America	399
Central America & Belize	24
Chile	6
Columbia, Panama & Ecuador	200
Cuba	702
Dominica, St.Vincent & St.Lucia	70
Dominican Republic	30
Dutch Antilles	20
French Guiana	51
Grenada	67
Gretare Antilles	2,421
Guadeloupe	291
Haiti	864
Jamaica	748
Lesser Antilles	1,614
Louisana	28
Martinique	366
Mexica	200
Peru	95
Puerto Rico	77
Surinam & Guyana	480
Trinidad & Tobago	22
Venezuela	121
Virgin Islands	35

Percentage of the population descended from slaves c. 1950

Brazil	30
Columbia	1
Cuba & West Indies	15
Ecuador	1
Panama	1
USA	30
Venezuela	1

Slave exports from Africa 1450-1900

Period	Volume	Per cent
1450-1600	367,000	3.1
1601-1700	1,868,000	16.0
1701-1800	6,133,000	52.4
1801-1900	3,330,000	28.5
Total	11,698,000	100.0

Atlantic slave trade 1701-1800

Carrier	Total
Danish	73,900
Dutch	350,900
English	2,532,300
French	1,180,300
North American	194,200
Portuguese	1,796,300
Other (Swedish, Brandenburger)	5,000
Total	6,132,900

Sex distribution of exported slaves in the nineteenth century

Category	number	per cent
Children	34,863	26.0
Women	28,847	21.5
Men	70,348	52.5
Total	134,058	100.0
Women as % Adults		29.1
Men as % Adults		70.9

Slaves from the Bight of Biafra captured by the British Navy and liberated in Sierra Leone, 1821-39.

Slave prices, Bight of Benin (1790s-1860s) based on £ sterling, 1913

Period	Price	%Change
1790s	22	–
1800s	17	–23
1810s	14	–18
1820s	16	+15
1830s	14	–13
1840s	14	–
1850s	12	–14
1860s	11	–8

Bibliography and Further Reading

The Ancient World

The Slave Systems of Greek and Roman Antiquity,
W. L. Westermann, Philadelphia, 1955
Greek and Roman Slavery, Thomas Wiedemann, London, 1981
Ancient Slavery and Modern Ideology, M. Finley, London, 1980

Africa

Women and Slavery in Africa, C. Robertson & M. Kiein, Madison, 1983
The Golden Trade of the Moors, E. Bovill, Oxford, 1958
Slavery and African Life, P. Manning, Cambridge, 1990
Slavery in Africa, S. Miers & I. Kopytoff; Madison, 1977
Transformations in Slavery, P. Lovejoy, Cambridge, 1983
The Atlantic Slave Trade, A Census, P. D. Curtin, Madison, 1969
Africa Remembered, P. D. Curtin, Madison, 1967

The Americas

Maroon Societies: Rebel Slave Communities in the Americas,
Richard Price ed., New York, 1973
The Masters and the Slaves, Gilberto Freyre, New York, 1971
The Transatlantic Slave Trade, James A. Rawley, New York, 1981
"Myne Uwne Ground" Race and Freedom on Virginia's Eastern Shore, 1640-1676,
T. H. Breen & Stephen Innes, New York, 1980
Roll, Jordan, Roll: The World the Slaves Made, Eugene D. Genovese, New York, 1972
Liverpool, the African Slave Trade, and Abolition,
Roger Anstey & P. E. H. Hair eds., Liverpool, 1989
Britain and the Ending of the Slave Trade, Suzanne Miers, London, 1975
Abolitionism, Herbert Aptheker, Boston, 1989
Black Union Soldiers in the Civil War, Hondon B. Hargrove,
Jefferson North Carolina, 1988
Caribbean Slave Society and Economy: A Student Reader, H. Beckles & V. Shepherd eds.,
Kingston Jamaica, 1991

Index